John Newton Stearns

Merry's Gems of Prose and Poetry

John Newton Stearns

Merry's Gems of Prose and Poetry

ISBN/EAN: 9783744685450

Printed in Europe, USA, Canada, Australia, Japan

Cover: Foto ©Thomas Meinert / pixelio.de

More available books at **www.hansebooks.com**

FRONTISPIECE.

MERRY'S GEMS

OF

Prose and Poetry.

EDITED BY
UNCLE MERRY.

NEW-YORK:

H. DAYTON, No. 36 HOWARD STREET.

INDIANAPOLIS, IND.: ASHER & CO.

1860.

CONTENTS.

	PAGE
THE Old Homestead	13
Anecdote of Daniel Webster	21
The Simple Truth	25
Life and Death	29
String of Pearls	30
Truth	34
The Nautilus	35
Fred's Visit to the Country	36
Good Night	41
Gentle Words—Loving Smiles	42
William Tell	43
Dry Clouds	45
The Great Chinese Puzzle	46
The Perils of Fishing	54
My Home	61
To Day	61
Leap Frog	62
The Butterfly	64
There is a Silver Lining to every Cloud	65
Harry Know-Nothing	66
The Child and the Angel	71
Story of the Two Millers	72
Timothy Fennel's Reflections	75
The Plough Boy	79
Spelling the Dictionary	81
On a Good Dog Called "Watch."	85
Old Whittemore Hill	86
An "Ax to Grind."	90
Scene in a Country School-House	91
Sweet will be our Rest	92
Look at Home	93
The Practical Joker	94
The Sunbeam's Mission	97
Kindness	98
The Seige of Belgrade	100

	PAGE.
April	101
Guess What?	103
Winter	106
The Hyacinth	108
Only Waiting	111
Young Men	113
Echo Answering	114
Chickens	115
The Way to do It	115
Tobacco	116
Reading	117
Just Too Late	118
Positive and Comparative	121
Life	122
Hops and Beans	123
The Fly	125
Little Dog Toby, and the White Pitcher	126
The Two Worlds	128
Little Graves	129
A Hint for the Boys	130
Never Give Up	132
Read this Boys	133
The Other Home	136
Kite Flying	137
The Bible	138
Perseverance—its Value	139
John Randolph Outdone	142
Whistling	143
The First Snow of the Season	145
The Family Unbroken	146
The Drunkard's Will	147
Helping Mother	148
Franklin's Mode of Lending Money	150
Cold Water Song	150
Drawing	153
Little by Little	155
What Saith the Fountain?	156
Advice to Youth	157
The Way to be Happy	158
The Chinese Opium Smoker	159
Teaching Under Difficulties	165
Work but don't Worry	167
The Wreath	168

CONTENTS.

	PAGE.
The Souhegan River	171
Try, Try Again	182
Bye-and-Bye	173
Sunshine	174
Our School-Time Hours	175
The Household "Good-Night."	176
The Life I'd Live	178
The Death I'd Die	179
Charade	180
What is a Year?	181
The Dogs	183
Cold Water	186
A "Strange" Preacher	187
Farmer's Boys	189
Address to Lake Ery	190
The Merry Heart	191
Little Red Riding-Hood	193
The Cabin Boy	194
The Request	196
When one Won't Quarrel Two Can't	198
Brilliants	199
Little Things	200
The Sublime of Nonsense	201
Not Time Enough	203
All About Eyes	204
Angry Words	205
Our Little Angel	206
Number of Stars	208
Voices	209
By-and-By	209
An Evening with Papa	210
Song of the Tree Toad	214
The Comforts of Playing "Hookie."	217
Pleasure and Duty	219
Telling Mother	220
Tell-tale Face	222
To the Suspensbin Bridge at Niagary	223
The Stone in the Pond	224
History of a Flower	226
Life's Smiles	230
Wants his Land Warrant	235
Rose and the Flower	237
Top Philosophy	240

ENGRAVINGS.

	PAGE
THE Old Homestead	14
Chinese Ancestral Tablet	16
Daniel Webster	21
String of Pearls	30
Fred's Visit to the Country	36
The Old Mill	38
Good Night	41
Tell steering the Boat on the Rocks	44
The Rescue	58
Leap-Frog	62
The Butterfly	64
Coming out of the Little End of the Horn	70
The Old Mill	72
The Plough Boy	79
The School Boys	82
Old Whittemore Hill	86
The Noisy Children just let loose from School	89
Sweet will be our Rest	92
April	101
Winter	106
Only Waiting	111
The Chickens	115
Just too Late	118
Little Graves	129
Kite Flying	137

PAGE

The News Boy.. 139
December 144
Helping Mother....................................... 148
Learning to Draw..................................... 152
The Fountain... 156
The Chinese Opium Smoker............................. 159
Chinese Mandarin..................................... 162
Teaching under Difficulties.......................... 165
The Wreath... 168
Sunshine... 174
The Household "Good Night."........................... 176
The Dogs in the Parlor............................... 182
Cold Water... 186
Little Red Riding-Hood............................... 192
The Request.. 196
Brilliants... 199
All About Eyes....................................... 204
Our Little Angel..................................... 206
An Evening with Papa................................. 210
Song of the Tree Toad................................ 214
The Blow... 218
The Stone in the Pond................................ 224
Flowers 226
The Indian... 234
Top Philosophy....................................... 240

PREFACE.

WE here present to our young friends a choice
selection of prose and poetry, which we hope
they will enjoy and find useful. We call them
"gems," because we think them all pure in sentiment
and well adapted to the comprehension and instruction of our young friends, for whom they are intended. When we were young, we took great pleasure
in reading such pieces, and in committing them to
memory. We have often passed a whole evening
very agreeably, repeating what we had thus learned,
while our brothers and sisters would take their
turns with us, vieing with us, to see who could recite
the greatest number of pieces. We often do it now
with our children, and find great pleasure in it.
The greater part of our stories of this kind, are
those which we laid up in our younger days, and
we send out this little volume, partly to furnish to
our young friends the means of enjoying the same
kind of pleasure. Many of the pieces here brought
together, are worthy, we think, to be committed to
memory, and recited at the family meetings, and

other occasions, where more active and boisterous amusements would be out of place. Besides being agreeable, it is a very profitable exercise. It strengthens the memory, and improves the taste. It assists, very much, in the cultivation of a good style of writing and of conversation, by furnishing a variety of choice expressions for the thoughts you wish to convey. We would earnestly recommend to all our young friends, as an important part of their education, to cultivate a love of poetry—to commit to memory, and often repeat, the choicest and best pieces ; always taking pains to recite them well, with proper tone and emphasis, so as to give every word its just force and expression.

The same remarks will apply to good selections of prose. There are many passages of rare force and beauty, which, like texts of Scripture, will never wear out, and never lose their value as gems of thought set in jewels of expression ; which it will be found very useful to have always at the tongue's end. If any such are found in this little book, which shall commend themselves to our young friends as worthy to be remembered, and as well as read, we shall be satisfied that we have done well in bringing them together in this form. If they only amuse, or entertain, they will not be wholly useless.

THE OLD HOMESTEAD.

ALL me not romantic, though I speak of the many pleasant recollections which cluster around the Old Homestead, and come thronging up from the days of childhood often as we re-visit it in the after years. The dear Old Homestead—where we first saw the light and first learned to know the looks and tones of love — where kind parents watched over us with yearning affection, and where a whole troup of fond brothers and sisters used to mingle together in the sweet fellowship of domestic bliss ; where we remembered and kept our birthdays. How the heart turns back to this hallowed spot, from all its various wanderings! How it lingers about the old associations, after years of absence, as if the cherished objects of the past would come back to its embrace and live again! It

Oh, spare the Old Homestead,
'Tis dear to me yet ;
The home of my childhood
I ne'er can forget.

is only after absence, separation, and loss that we
fully know how precious to the soul were its first
loves, and how important the influences and sur-
roundings of its early days.

But how changed is everything about the dear old
place now! I love it still, but am pained, as well
as glad to re-visit it. The garden we thought so
much of is grown over with weeds. The paths 're
so often trod are overgrown with grass. The house
itself is changed. The dear old kitchen, the heart
of the mansion, has been made smaller, to give
room for a cosy little sitting-room at one end. It

may be cosy and convenient to the new-comers, but it is not the spacious old kitchen, where all the work of the house could be done and all the family sit round the ample fire of hickory logs, and where there was always room enough for "blindman's buff," "hide and seek," "puss in the corner," and other kindred philosophies of those blessed days at home, to say nothing of huskings, molasses candy scrapes, etc., etc.

The old south room is not much changed. How many scenes come back upon memory as I open the door—the prayer-meetings, the social gatherings of family friends, the thanksgiving parties, the birthday festivals, and the eager gathering of the whole group to listen to the last letter from the loved and absent in China, to hear of the strange people there, their idolatries, their customs, and their curious works. Here, in the engraving, you see them listening to an explanation of a Chinese ancestral tablet, which had just arrived, among other curiosities, from that distant land.

Yet some things remain as of old. The spacious barn is there, and the long shed, protecting the north side of the yard. The old hill in the distance, with its straggling fringe of half-blasted trees, and its solemn look toward heaven. But more than all, the bright sparkling brook, that babbled along the edge of the garden, and sauntered down into the valley, as if it were in no hurry to get through; though, after leaving it, it would rush on to the river, as if ambitious to find its way to the ocean. And yet, after all, the brook was changed too. It sang the same old tune, but it seemed to be set to different words. The air was familiar, but my heart could not *chime in* as of old. What was the matter?

This brook had something more than sparkles and babblings to commend it. It was perfectly alive

CHINESE ANCESTRAL TABLET.

with trout, and I used to know just where to find, and just how to take, them. Often, after the day's work was done, or when it rained too hard to "work in the garden," I would take my pole and try my hand for a morning meal. I became familiar with every hole and nook where "most the trout did congregate," and almost with every shining little fellow among them, and could generally tell when one was large enough to be promoted from the brook to the table. Many a time have I put back into the stream some venturesome little fellow who had come unbidden to my hook, thus giving him opportunily to grow worthy of the dignity of being eaten.

Well do I remember how my venerated father valued his brook, talking of it as his "meat-tub in the meadow," and how he was always successful in bringing something out of it, when others could catch nothing.

But this is all past. To-

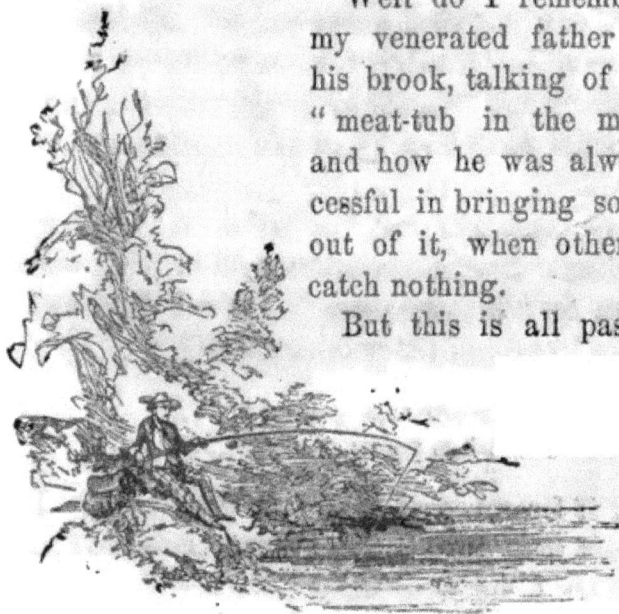

day I took a line and went down to see if they would
remember the old friend who had not forgotten them.
It rained, but I took my old stand on the bridge
and threw my line. A moment of watching—then
—"flap!" there he comes, as fine and plump a fellow as ever gladdened the eye of old Izaac. They
knew me—they did. In half an hour I was on my
way up with a goodly string of them, all eager to
be broiled for my breakfast.

The old school-house in the distance caught my
eyes. What scenes came flitting along as memory
carried me back to the good old days when, within
those narrow walls, the "young idea" first learned
"to shoot," sometimes overshooting the mark, and
sometimes "going off in a squib," or "flashing in
the pan!" Those "spelling-schools!" Ah! what a
spell of ambitious rivalry was on us, as we strove
to see who could remain longest "standing up!"
Why, I could spell five times as well then as I can
now.

After the last one was "*spelled down*" came the
declamations. I well remember my first trial, when
called out to "*say my piece.*" How I trembled!
How fully I realized the good sense of

> "You'd scarce expect one of my age
> To speak in public on the stage!"

I wonder if I can repeat that first piece now! No
sooner said than done. Down went fishing rod and
fish, and up I mounted on an old familiar stump,

made " my bow to the whole world and the rest of
mankind," and addressed myself to Niagara thus :

> I wonder how long you've been a roaring'
>   At this tremendous rate !
> I wonder if all you've been pourin'
>   Could be ciphered on a slate !
> I wonder how such a thunderin' sounded
>   When all New York was woods !
> 'Spose likely some Indians have been drownded,
>   When rains had raised your floods !
> I wonder if wild stags and buffaloes
>   Haven't stood where now I stand !
> Well 'spose (being scared at first) they'd stubbed
>   their toes,
>   I wonder where they'd land !
> I wonder if that rainbow has been shinin'
>   Since sunrise at creation—
> And this waterfall been underminin'
>   With constant spatteration !
>   'hat Moses never mentioned ye, I've wondered,
>   While other things describin' !
> My conscience ! how ye must have foamed and thundered,
>   When the deluge was subsidin' !
> " My thoughts are strange," magnificent, and deep,
>   " When I look down to thee,"
> O ! what a glorious place for washing sheep
>   Niagara will be !
> And oh ! what a tremendous water-power
>   Is wasted o'er its edge—
> One man might furnish all the world with flour
>   With a single privilege !
> I wonder how many times the lakes have all
>   Been emptied over here !

Why Clinton didn't fill the Great Canal
  Up here, I think is queer.
The thoughts are " very strange " which crowd my brain,
  " While I look up to thee,"
Such thoughts I never expect to have again
  To all eternity !

As my old pine-wood audience did not see fit to clap or stamp, I stamped down from my stump, clapped up my fish, and started homeward. Everything seemed more familiar than ever.

Even the squirrels knew me as I walked along, and skipped about the old trees as if they knew that, with the fishing-rod in one hand and an ample supply of trout in the other, I should not be likely to ask them to smell my powder.

I went out to the hay-field. It was the same old work, but the fun was all worked out of it. The boys were not there—nor—*the girls.* But the hay went in, and so did I, as soon as I decently could. The old adage says, " Make hay while the sun shines." I say, make hay at home, and this is not home now.

ANECDOTE OF DANIEL WEBSTER.

I WELL remember hearing my father tell the following anecdote, illustrative of the early genius of that great man whose loss a mighty nation mourns :

Ebenezer Webster, the father of Daniel, was a farmer. The vegetables in his garden had suffered considerably from the depredations of a woodchuck, whose hole and habitation were near the premises

Daniel, some ten or twelve years old, and his older
brother Ezekiel had set a trap, and finally succeeded
in catching the trespasser. Ezekiel proposed to kill
the animal, and end at once all further trouble from
him ; but Daniel looked with compassion upon his
meek, dumb captive, and offered to let him again go
free. The boys could not agree, and each appealed
to their father to decide the case. "Well, my
boys," said the old gentleman, "I will be the judge.
There is your prisoner, (pointing to the woodchuck,)
and you shall be the counsel, and plead the case
for and against his liberty."

Ezekiel opened the case with a strong argument,
urging the mischievous nature of the criminal, the
great harm he had already done, said that much
time and labor had been spent in his capture, and
now, if he was suffered to live and go again at
large, he would renew his depredations, and be
cunning enough not to suffer himself to be caught
again, but that he ought now to be put to death ;
that his skin was of some value, but that to make
the most of him they could, it would not repay half
the damage he had already done. His argument
was ready, practical, and to the point, and of much
greater length than our limits will allow us to
occupy in relating the story.

The father looked with pride upon his son, who
became a distinguished jurist in his manhood.
"Now, Daniel, it is your turn. I'll hear what you
have to say."

This was his first case. Daniel saw that the plea
of his brother had sensibly affected his father, the
judge ; and as his large, brilliant black eyes looked
upon the soft, timid expression of the animal, and he
saw it tremble with fear in its narrow prison-
house, his heart swelled with pity, and he appealed
with eloquent words that the captive might again
go free. God, he said, had made the woodchuck ;
he had made him to live, to enjoy the bright sunlight, the pure air, the free fields and woods. God
had not made him or any thing in vain ; the woodchuck had as much right to life as any other living
thing ; he was not a destructive animal, as the wolf
and the fox were ; he simply ate a few common
vegetables, of which they had a plenty and could
well spare a part ; he destroyed nothing except the
little food he needed to sustain his humble life ; and
that little food was as sweet to him, and as neces-
cary to his existence, as was to them the food upon
his mother's table. God furnished their own food ;
He gave them all they possessed ; and would they
not spare a little for the dumb creature who really
had as much right to his small share of God's
bounty, as they themselves had to their portion?
Yea, more ; the animal had never violated the laws
of his nature or the laws of God, as man often did,
but strictly followed the simple, harmless instincts
he had received from the hand of the Creator of all
things. Created by God's hand, he had a right, a
right from God, to life, to food, to liberty ; and

they had no right to deprive him of either. He alluded to the mute but the earnest pleadings of the animal for that life, as sweet, as dear to him, as their own was to them ; and the just judgement they might expect if, in selfish cruelty and cold heartlessness, they took the life they could not restore again, the life that God alone had given.

During this appeal the tears had started to the old man's eyes, and were fast running down his sunburnt cheeks ; every feeling of a father's heart was stirred within him ; he saw the future greatness of his son before his eyes ; he felt that God had blessed him in his children beyond the lot of common men ; his pity and sympathy were awakened by the eloquent words of compassion, and the strong appeal for mercy ; and, forgetting the judge in the man and the father, he sprang from his chair, (while Daniel was in the midst of his argument, without thinking he had already won the case,) and turning to his older son, dashing the tears from his eyes, exclaimed, " ZEKE, ZEKE, YOU LET THAT WOODCHUCK GO !"

———

A ROMAN clergyman lately illustrated the necessity of corporeal punishment for the correction of juvenile depravity, with the remark that " the child, when once started in a course of evil conduct was like a locomotive on the wrong track, it takes a switch to get it off."

THE SIMPLE TRUTH.

EMILY and Julia Carlton, one day when their mother was gone out, enticed Brutus, the great fat house-dog, into the parlor, and began a game of romps with him. Now Brutus was old and lazy, and did not like to be pulled about by the little girls ; so he ran under the table, and sideboard, and sofa, to get away from them, while they pursued, clapping their hands and laughing. But they did not laugh long : for Brutus, in trying to escape, overturned a stand upon which stood a glass globe containing gold and silver fish. The globe was of course broken, and the poor little fish, gasping and struggling, lay scattered upon the carpet.

The children were at first too much frightened to speak ; but Julia soon found her tongue, and exclaimed, " Poor little fish ! poor little fish ! O, what will mother say to us ?"

" Poor little fish !" echoed Emily " they will all die. O, what shall we do ?"

" Mother will be very angry with us, and will punish us," said Julia.

" She will be displeased with us for calling Brutus into the parlor ; but she will not punish us if we tell her the truth."

" Yes, she will, I know," said Julia, " She won't let us go to cousin Harriet's party to-morrow."

"Well, I shall not be so sorry for that as I am for the gold fish."

"Mother needn't know we brought Brutus into the parlor, Emily. We can run into the garden to play, and she won't find it out."

"O Julia! you would not be so wicked."

"It would not be wicked," said Julia. "I do not mean to tell a lie."

"But you mean to *act* a lie; and mother has told us, a great many times, *that* is just as bad as *telling* one. It would be a great deal worse than calling Brutus into the parlor, because then we did not *mean* to do wrong. Mother likes to have us tell the simple truth, and I shall tell it to her, and then she won't punish us."

Mrs. Carlton came in while Emily was speaking "O, my poor gold fish!" she exclaimed, and hastened forward to the kitchen. She returned in an instant with a bowl of water, and carefully took up the fish and put them into it.

"They do not move," she said, after she had watched them awhile. "They are quite dead." She then turned to her daughters, and desired to know how the accident had happened.

"Brutus threw down the stand, mother," said Julia.

"How came Brutus in the parlor?" asked Mrs. Carlton.

"He came in—at—the—open door—I suppose," stammered Julia.

" Brutus knows he is not permitted to come into the parlor, and he must have been called, or he would not have entered it now. But how happened he to throw down the stand ?"

" He ran against it, mother."

" Brutus is usually a careful dog. I think he would not have thrown down the stand unless he had been driven or forced against it. Come, Emily, you always tell a straightforward story. Let me hear how it was."

" We called Brutus into the parlor, because we wanted him to play with us ; but he did not like to play, and he crept under the sideboard, and table, and sofa, to get away from us. We drove him out, and laughed, and clapped our hands ; and I suppose he was frightened, for he ran, and we ran after him, till he hit the stand and threw it down."

" How beautiful is truth!" said Mrs. Carlton, as she stooped to kiss Emily.

" I told the truth, too," said Julia, with tears in her eyes.

" Not the *simple truth*, and the whole truth, my dear. You merely did not tell a falsehood ; but you did all you could do, without telling one, to throw the blame on somebody, or something, besides yourself. Emily, on the contrary, kept nothing back ; neither did she try to excuse herself by ac- cusing Brutus and the open door ; but with the per- fect frankness and fairness of her character, told the truth, and the whole truth. Now tell me, my dear, what have you ever gained by your habit of keeping back part of the truth, when you fear the whole of it will bring you into trouble."

Julia was obliged to answer, "Nothing."

"And what have you lost?"

"Nothing, mother."

"Is the confidence of your friends 'nothing,' my dear child?"

Julia had often felt pain from not being believed and trusted, as her sister Emily was; and she burst into tears.

"You know, my dear Julia," said Mrs. Carlton, "I love you too tenderly ever to give you pain but for your good; and I believe, if the pain you suffer now should induce you to correct this fault, you will hereafter thank me for inflicting it. Did you ever hear what was a wise man's reply, when asked what a man gains by telling a falsehood?"

"No, mother."

"It was, 'Not to be believed when he speaks the truth.' *Remember this;* and let it teach you to speak the simple truth in future."

BOYS, did you ever think that this great world with all its wealth and woe, with all its mines and mountains, its oceans, seas and rivers, steamboats and ships, railroads and steam printing presses, magnetic telegraphs, etc., will soon be given over to the hands of the boys of the present age? Believe it, and look abroad upon the inheritance, and get ready to enter upon you duties.

LIFE AND DEATH.

" WHAT is life, father ?"—A battle, my child,
  Where the strongest lance may fail—
Where the wariest eye may be beguiled,
  And the stoutest heart may quail—
Where the foes are gathered on every hand,
  And rest not day or night,
And the feeble little ones must stand
  In the thickest of the fight.

" What is death, father ?"—The rest, my child,
  When the strife and the toil are o'er—
The angel of God, who, calm and mild,
  Says we need fight no more—
Who driveth away the demon bands
  Bids the din of the battle cease,
Takes the banner and spear from failing hands,
  And proclaims an eternal peace.

  Let *me* die, father. I tremble and fear
  To fall in that terrible strife !"—
The crown must be won for Heaven, dear,
  In the battle field of Life.
Courage ! thy foes may be strong and tried,
  But he loveth the weak and small ;
The angels of heaven are on thy side,
  And God is over all !

HOME.

THOUGH care and trouble may be mine,
  As down life's path I roam,
I'll heed them not while still I have
  A world of love at home.

STRING OF PEARLS.

I SAT at my window and looked down upon the river, which, swollen by recent rains, rushed on toward the sea. The trees and green banks were no longer reflected in its waters. It was in too much haste to picture them as it passed.

On, on it rushed, and every thing which rested on its waves was borne with it away. Rafts went by guided by men who knew all the dangers of the rapid stream, and scorned them. A little boat, loosened from its moorings, came floating along, to be dashed in pieces with the logs and uprooted trees. Fascinated by the scene, I gazed till the noise of the waters became a dull murmur, and the river, and banks, and quiet village beyond faded away. I slept, and as I slept the scene before me mingled with my thoughts. I stood on the banks of the river, not now dashing and rushing on, but calm and quiet, gentle ripples only disturbing its surface ; and floating slowly down the stream, came a little boat. In it was a manly youth, who, half reclining, guided with ease the little bark ; nearer and nearer he came, so that I observed that ever and anon he turned his head, and raised his hand, as if to receive something from some one above him. I looked more earnestly, and saw dimly, faintly revealed, an angel figure bending over him, and offering to him a string of pearls. The youth received them with a careless laugh, and after holding them for a moment, dropped them one by one in the bright waters. Still the angel hand continued to supply him, and still he threw the precious gems as carelessly away. What, thought I, is this only play—I will know the meaning of this. Then I saw another form beside the youth, and as he threw the pearls away, this angel caught them from the gathering waters, and strung them again. The face of this angel was sad, and he looked carefully at each precious gem, as if to see whether it had received any impress from the youth. Then I saw that six of these gems were pearls beautifully set with twenty-four smaller gems, but the seventh, which was also surrounded with twenty-four gems, was a diamond. I looked then to see how the youth would receive the diamond ; surely, thought I, he will prize it more than the rest. But no, he seemed glad indeed to receive the gem, but he threw it away more hastily than any of the others. Then I saw that the sad-faced angel talked with the young man, and showed him the long string of gems which he had gathered from the waters, and the youth's face, too, grew sad for a moment, and as he received another pearl, he held it more carefully, and even attempted to engrave something upon it, for I saw that these gems were already prepared to receive the letters which the young man was expected to mark upon them. Then I rejoiced to think that these beautiful gems were no longer to be thrown carelessly away; but, alas! the youth tried for a moment, then cast the pearl overboard with an impatient—"'Tis useless, I can't trouble myself so."

Now the boat had floated very near me, so I called to the youth, and asked him whither he was floating, and why he threw away so carelessly such beautiful gems.

"Why, you see, I know I shall have plenty more of them; as long as I float on this river I can have them, and I throw them away because I can only keep one at a time, and there is nothing different in them. I can make them different by engraving certain words upon them; indeed, I am told, that is what they are given to me for, but it's too much trouble; and if I begin now, I shall have to write a great many before I get through, I'm afraid."

"But, when will you get through?" said I.

"Oh, I don't know exactly," replied the youth;

" that depends upon the length of this river, and the swiftness of the current; it may be a great while, and it may not."

" And where do you go then?" was my question.

The young man shuddered. " There is a dreary, boundless ocean then," he answered, " but I don't want to think of that."

" But," I persisted, " why does the pale figure by your side keep gathering up those stones, and placing them on the string?"

" That is to see how many I have written on. They tell me that when I get to the mouth of this river, I may reach a beautiful country, and live there; but it all depends on what I write on those stones, so there isn't much prospect of my getting there;" and he laughed—a hollow, affected laugh.

" Why don't you write on them," asked I, " since you gain so much by it?"

" Oh, 'tis too much trouble. Here it goes "—and with these words he tossed over the pearl he had been holding while talking to me, and raised up his hand for another.

I looked wonderingly after him, as he floated on out of my sight. Then I thought, " I will ascend this high hill, and watch that little boat;" so I climbed the hill, and behold, from the top, I could see the whole course of the river, and far on I saw the little boat. · The waters here were no longer calm, there were rapids and rocks to avoid, and the young man no longer looked carelessly, but anxious-

ly watched, peering forward into the darkness, to
see what was coming. It needed much care to
keep his boat afloat, and sometimes I fancied it was
lost, and then I would see it rise on the waves, and
struggle on again. Still I could see that his hand
was raised for the pearls, and I fancied that he held
them longer, and looked at them more earnestly
than he did before. So he went forward—wrathful
waves around—and the deep surging of the unknown
sea distinctly heard, as he came nearer and nearer
to it. A startling scream, and the boat gave a sudden plunge, and when I looked, there dimly, in the
lowering darkness of the great ocean, I saw the poor
man's figure, struggling with the waves. His boat
was a wreck. There was one flash of light, and by
it methought I saw two angel figures weeping bitterly, flying upward, bearing with them the string
of pearls.

TRUTH.

ALWAYS speak the truth. Nothing will so exalt
the individual as virtue, and virtue cannot be
perfected without an understanding regard to truth.
The person whose word is not sacred to himself,
and sure to others, lives in a very degraded sphere
of life. The trustworthy dog stands more than on a
level with him in the sphere of being, and is deserv-
ing of more honor. But the individual of truthful
lips, lives in an exalted sphere of life, having the
confidence of all around him.

THE NAUTILUS.

THE Nautilus floats on the azure deep,
She opens her sail, when the wild winds sleep,
When the sun shines bright, and dolphins play
Then moves she along like a lady gay,
      For a lady is she
      Of the deep deep sea,
And nought is so pretty or half so free
As the ocean's fair gem of purity.

In the pride of her beauty she moves along,
And welcomed she is by the mariner's song,
For when on the ocean they see the sail
They cheerfully sing and wish her well;
      For a lady is she
      Of the deep deep sea,
And nought is so pretty or half so free
As the ocean's fair gem of purity.

When hollow winds whistle and billows roar,
She takes in her sail, and you see her no more,
Yet when the waves sleep and tempest is gone
Yet lady-like still she moveth along;
      For a lady is she
      Of the deep deep sea,
And nought is so pretty or half so free
As the ocean's fair gem of purity.

Like the Nautilus—may each of us sail,
May our vessel of life be free from a gale,
When the tempests of life, and its billows are gone
May we float like the Nautilus merrily on;
      For a lady is she
      Of the deep deep sea,
And nought is so pretty or half so free
As the ocean's fair gem of purity.

FRED'S VISIT TO THE COUNTRY.

FRED DANFORTH had always had a pleasant
home, a kind father, an affectionate mother, and
a darling sister, named Helen, who was only two
years his senior, and as fond of sport and play as
his little heart could wish. Fred and his pretty
sister loved each other dearly—they rarely quar-

reled, for their mother was always near to warn
them against all angry words,—and it was a pretty
sight to see the little Helen, throw down her skip-
ping rope or ball, when Fred grew tired of listening to his mother's stories, and try to amuse him by
bringing him bright flowers, or reading to him from
some of the books she kept in the little bookcase
her father had given her for a birthday present.

Fred often thought and said, that he never could
be happy away from his kind parents, and little sister ; but when he was about ten years old, his
Aunt Clara, went away some fifty miles into the
country to visit her sister, and took Fred for company on the journey. It made him feel so much like
a man to go on this first trip, that he quite forgot
that he was to leave all his dear friends behind, till
the time came to bid them good bye. Then, I am
afraid, the tears filled his eyes, and there was a big
lump in his throat that made him feel as if he was
choking—but in a little while he got over this, and
enjoyed the swift ride in the cars very much indeed.

Fred's uncle lived upon a farm, just out of the
village of Monticel'o. It was nearly dark when the
travelers reached the place, but Fred had time, after
supper, to run about a little, and see what the place
was like. He found a famous great tree on the
green before the door, and thought he would ask his
uncle, the next day, if he might have a swing put up
there. Then there was a meeting-house a little way
off, and a few cottages, and close beside the road,

and only a little distance from the great tree, was a small brook, with an arched stone bridge over it, that pleased him very much. As he walked down that way, a man came up, leading two of the farm horses—one white, and the other black. He let go of the bridles, and waited for them to drink. Fred began to talk with him, and soon found out that his name was Mike, and that the black horse, was named "Dolly," while the white one answered to the name of "Snowball." Mike put him on old Dolly's back, and he rode up to the house in high glee, just as his aunt was coming to the door to call him to bed.

The next morning Fred was up early, eager to take a long walk, with his kind aunt, who knew all

THE OLD MILL.

the beautiful places on the farm. She led him down
a long and narrow lane, till they came suddenly
upon an old windmill, that was a new and strange
sight to the boy. They stood upon a little bank
just beyond the mill, looking down at the brook
beyond, and at a little boat that was gliding along
there, like a living thing. Fred clapped his hands
and exclaimed:

"Oh, Auntie, we must have a sail before I go
back!"

"Yes," said his kind aunt, "we will have one the
day after to-morrow, if the day is fair. Mike shall
take us out to Still Pond, where the white lilies
grow, and if you pick some for Helen, they can be
kept pretty fresh till we see her. Now look at the
mill, Fred."

Fred looked. The miller had opened the door,
and was standing on the steps, and up over the roof,
the sails were going slowly round, like long arms
stretched out in the air. Fred wanted a ride on
one of them, but his aunt laughed so heartily at the
idea, that he gave it up a moment after, and was
quite willing to exchange it, for one with Mike, who
now came jolting by, with a high wagon and old
Snowball, and stopped to take them in.

Fred thought that was one of the happiest weeks
he had ever spent. He had a nice swing and a ride
now and then on old Dolly—and then for play-
mates, he had a funny little black and white puppy
named "Jip, and all the hens, and chickens, and

geese, and turkeys on the farm. And then, the day before he went away, he had such a famous sail with his aunt, and Mike, in his uncle's boat. They went a long way out on the pond, and filled the bottom of the boat with the whitest and sweetest lilies he had ever seen. His aunt wrapped them up carefully in wet paper the next morning, and after Fred had said good-bye to every body and every thing on the farm, they were whirled away again in the rattling cars, towards home.

They got there just in time for tea, and Fred cried for joy when he felt his mother's arms around him, and Helen's kiss upon his cheek. The little girl was delighted with the fragrant lilies, and Fred had so much to tell her of the wonderful things he had seen, that his tongue ran faster than a race horse. Mrs. Danforth has promised both her children a visit to the old farm-house during the next summer, if they are good and kind to each other, and Master Fred is making great calculations about the "fun" he will have then, with Helen to keep him company.

An Irish piper, who now and then indulged in a glass too much, was accosted by a gentleman with, "Pat, what makes your face so red?" Please your honor," said Pat, "I always blush when I spake to a gintleman.

GOOD NIGHT.

"Good night, dear mamma !" a little girl said,
"I'm going to sleep in my trundle bed ;
Good night dear papa, little brother and siss !"
And to each one the innocent gave a sweet kiss
"Good night little darling," her fond mother said—
"But remember, before you lie down in your bed,
With a heart full of love, and a tone soft and mild,
To breathe a short prayer to Heaven, dear child."
"Oh, yes, dear mother !" said the child, with a nod,
"I love, oh ! I love to say good night to God !"

Kneeling down, "My Father in Heaven," she said
"I thank thee for giving me this nice little bed ;
For though mamma told me she brought it for me,
She says that everything good comes from Thee ;
I thank Thee for keeping me safe through the day.;
I thank Thee for teaching me, too, how to pray ;"

Then bending her sweet little head with a nod,
"Good night my dear Father, my Maker and God
Should I never again on earth open mine eyes,
I pray Thee to give me a home in the skies!"

'Twas an exquisite sight as she meekly knelt there,
With her eyes raised to Heaven, her hands clasped in
  prayer;
And I thought of the time when the Saviour, in love,
Said, " Of such is the kingdom of Heaven above;"
And I inwardly prayed that my own heart the while,
Might be cleansed of its bitterness, freed from its guile;
Then she crept into bed, that beautiful child,
And was soon lost in slumber so calm and so mild,
That we listened in vain for the sound of her breath
As she lay in the arms of the emblem of death.

GENTLE WORDS—LOVING SMILES.

THE sun may warm the grass of life,
 The dew the drooping flower,
And eyes grow bright that watch the light
 Of Autumn's opening hour—
But words that breathe of tenderness,
 And smiles we know are true
Are warmer than the summer time,
 And brighter than the dew.

It is not much the world can give,
 With all its subtle art,
And gold and gems are not the things
 To satisfy the heart;
But oh, if those who cluster round
 The altar and the hearth,
Have gentle words and loving smiles,
 How beautiful is earth!

WILLIAM TELL.

IN 1307, Switzerland was under the dominion of an Austrian tyrant, named Herman Gessler. The Swiss have always been a hard people for tyrants to manage, and this governor had his match with them. It seems he suspected they were not perfectly loyal. So one day, he ordered a hat to be raised on a pole, and commanded everybody to do homage to it, as if his own head were under it. Tell refused. He was arrested for disobedience, and the tyrant cruelly directed him to shoot an arrow at an apple placed on the head of his own son, or else to be dragged with his child to immedi- ate death. What a dreadful choice! Tell was a good archer, and he determined to try his skill, though at the eminent hazard of murdering his child. He raised the bow, took deliberate aim,— with a steady hand ; and wonderful to relate, cleft the apple in two without injuring his son! God aided that injured man—God indeed is ever on the side of the oppressed and against the oppressor. Tell had another arrow in his quiver ; and he de- clared that if he had hurt his child, that arrow would have been thrust through the heart of the tyrant.

This boldness was the occasion of his confine- ment ; and the governor, afraid of a rescue, carried him across the lake of Lucerne. But a violent

TELL STEERING THE BOAT ON THE ROCKS.

storm obliged Gessler, who knew that the prisoner was a good sailor, to entrust to him the helm of the vessel for the preservation of his own life. Tell, freed from his chains, steered the boat on a rock. That rock is still called by his name. He leaped ashore, unhurt, and escaped into mountains. That governor was afterwards shot by the hand of Tell ; and the Swiss roused to arms by the conduct of their hero, drove away their Austrian master, and established the independence of Switzerland. Nearly fifty years after this event, Willian Tell was drowned.

DRY CLOUDS.—Two boys among the blackberry bushes, some mile or two out of town, saw a cloud rising and heard a sound like thunder. One who was a little timid said to the other, " Come, Fred, let's go home—it thunders." The other, not wishing to return home so soon, denied that it thundered at all. Directly the rumbling noise was again borne on the freshening breeze. " What's that, then ?" inquired the other. " Why, Fred, don't you know what that is ? If you don't, I'll tell you. You know it has been dry weather for a long time. What clouds there are floating about are as dry as old sheep-skins, and when the wind blows it rattles them."

THE GREAT CHINESE PUZZLE.

MANY years ago, during the time of the third
dynasty of the Emperors of China, which com-
menced about the year 1,110, B. C., there reigned
over that country an Emperor named Ching. He
had an only daughter who was his greatest pride
and joy. She had a fair skin, with a delicate tinge
of pink on her fat cheeks ; her little eyes were bright
and sparkling, and her thick hair was black as the
raven's wing ; but her greatest beauty was her feet,
which were but *three inches long*.

This interesting maiden, Yang-te-Se, was loved by
a young Chinese named Hang-Ho, a youth beneath
her in birth and fortune. Now, as her father was
Emperor, or, as his subjects styled him, the "Son of
Heaven," he looked higher for a husband for his
daughter. Even the noblest in his realm were not
deemed worthy of her, and it was his hope that
some rich neighboring monarch would purchase her
for a large sum, so that he might then build himself,
for his summer residence, a beautiful kiosk on the
banks of the Yang-Kiang.

My young readers are all aware that the Chinese
are remarkably fond of puzzles, and that they are
famous for having furnished some of the most difficult that have ever been invented ; but I doubt if
any of you know the origin of the *Great Chinese
Puzzle*.

It is a pleasant summer's afternoon, and the great Ching has ordered some of the Mandarins (officers of state) to meet at his imperial palace, to consider a subject of great moment. There are assembled about a dozen men, all seated quietly upon the floor, smoking their pipes, while the Emperor is reclining upon a cushion.

"You all know," said he, "that I have been, for some time, wanting to marry my daughter?"

On hearing this, all the yellow Mandarins started, while their sharp black eyes twinkled, each thinking—"perhaps I can pay enough to buy me this pretty little wife."

"But one," he continued, "has dared to love her, who has not near money enough to pay her price; and for this boldness he must die!"

Then all the Mandarins dropped their pipes, and turned very pale, for each one knew that he had loved the Emperor's daughter. Hereupon, they all, with one bound, threw themselves at Ching's feet, and begged for their lives. A most ludicrous scene now presented itself. Imagine the Emperor, lying on the cushion, laughing immoderately, while his great officers are sprawling on the floor, screaming for mercy.

When they all became somewhat composed, the Emperor arose and said, "So, you love Yang-te-Se! Well, you ought all to die; but I will be merciful. You are none of you the one I mean, for you have never yet importuned me for her hand. There is one, however, who has not been as wise as you ; and, for his folly, he shall die. Go immediately and order him to be brought here. It is the young Hang-Ho."

As the Emperor uttered these words he waved his hand towards the door, and one of the Mandarins left the room to execute the order. In about an hour he returned, bringing quite a good looking young man, who, immediately upon entering, prostrated himself humbly before Ching.

"That is, indeed, the right position for you, my young fellow," said the Emperor ; "but do you know why you have been sent for ?"

"Yes ;" he replied, " to die for my love for Yang-te-Se ! sweet Yang-te-Se !" and as he murmured the maiden's name, he raised his eyes reproachfully towards her father.

"Impudence!" muttered the Emperor, flattered, however, that his young daughter was so well loved.

I must, before proceeding further, inform you that the Emperor Ching was a very ingenious man, fond of all sorts of tricks and amusing games ; and it was his greatest delight when any of his subjects invented any kind of puzzle, to be the first to discover the answer.

This same fondness for puzzles seems, ever since the days of Ching, to have characterised the Chinese nation, so that while in this country you are asked if you have read the last new book, in China you are asked if you have seen the last new puzzle —and if you have solved it.

" Will not your Majesty listen to my request ?"
said the young Hang-Ho.

" Yes ; if you will be quick and make it, for you
cannot live much longer."

" But it is a request for my life."

"Well, what price will you pay for it ?" asked
the Emperor, with a sarcastic laugh.

" I have," continued the young man, without
noticing this interruption, " a plan now in my head
of a new style of puzzle ; and if you, oh mighty
Ching, will promise me, that if you do not discover
the puzzle within thirty days from the time that I
present it to you, you will grant me my life—well
and good ; but if you will not promise this, then
your Majesty's eyes shall never behold the *Puzzle*.

This was a pretty bold tone for the young man to
assume, and the Mandarins looked on in astonish-
ment at seeing how calmly the Emperor bore it.
But Hang-Ho knew the ground on which he stood,
and that he was offering a great temptation.

Now, as I have said, the Emperor was very ingenious, and very apt at discovering all sorts of puzzles, so, he thought to himself—" the young man
will die in the end, for there can be no puzzle invented that I cannot find out in thirty days ; and
even if I should not happen to discover it within
that time, it will be better to give him his life than
to have this Great Puzzle lost to our nation." So
he promised Hang-Ho that he would grant his request, and a writing was immediately drawn up by

one of the Mandarins, to this effect, and signed by the Emperor Ching.

"And now, young man," he said, "to-morrow I shall expect to see this wonderful puzzle, on which hangs your life."

"Yes, most gracious monarch," replied the latter, as he bowed thrice and then left the apartment.

On the following morning, very early, Hang-Ho presented himself at the imperial palace. In his hand he held a small wooden box. He was immediately admitted into the presence of the monarch, who, advancing a few steps, said, "Well, my young man, have you got the puzzle?"

"Oh yes," replied Hang-Ho showing him the wooden box, which the Emperor took, and tried to open it. The box was very small—only about four inches square, and was composed of a number of pieces of sandal-wood, of different shades, shapes, and sizes, all neatly fitted together. After examining it very attentively, the Emperor looked up, his sharp black eyes twinkling with pleasure, and said:

"Well, well, Hang-Ho, this is indeed very prettily made, but you cannot puzzle me," and he pressed his finger against one of the squares, which immediately yielded to the touch, and one of the sides of the box flew out. The young man merely smiled, while the former continued, "but what are these?" and he took out seven geometrical figures, beautifully carved in ivory. Five of them were right-angled triangles of **various sizes, one was a** perfect square, and the other a rhomboid.

"These seven figures," replied the **young man,** when rightly placed together, will **form an** exact square."

The Emperor **was** deeply interested. He had **seen** many sorts **of** puzzles, but never anything of this description.

"I hope no one has seen this?" he inquired.

"No," replied the young man, "not a person in the kingdom except us two."

"That is well," added **the** Emperor. "Let it remain **a** secret for the present. Not even one of the ladies of the court must know this. Remember!" and he shook his finger warningly at Hang-Ho.

"You shall be obeyed," replied the youth, laying his hand on **his** heart, and bowing thrice, he left the Emperor Ching, as we will also, deeply in the study **of** the puzzle.

It is noised abroad through the kingdom that the Emperor is engaged in studying out a new puzzle, invented by the young Hang-Ho, and that, if the former discovers it within thirty days, it will cost the latter his life, and all because he has dared **to** love the pretty **Yang-te-Se;** and the **men** shake their heads, muttering, "**The** great Ching sets too high a price on his daughter. Poor Hang-Ho is lost."

But no, he is not lost! The thirty days have passed, and the Emperor has not solved the puzzle.

Again he assembles his Mandarins, and proclaims his failure, and, in their presence, he clasps the hand of the young Hang-Ho, saying, " You are a clever fellow, and I would like to reward you. Now, what do you wish for most ?"

"A wife," he replied earnestly, murmuring the name of " Yang-te-Se."

"How bold," whisper the Mandarins to each other ; " but he is a great man now, for he has invented a puzzle which even our sovereign cannot discover."

" Young man," replied the Emperor, "I will give you a chance, even for the hand of my daughter. I will present the puzzle to all the first young ladies of my kingdom, and if any one of them discovers the answer within thirty days, whoever she may be, you shall marry her. It is your only chance," he continued, seeing that Hang-Ho hesitated to reply. " Yang-te-Se shall try with the rest. Will you agree to this ?"

" I will," replied the young man, a flush of hope rising to his cheeks.

Now, let us visit the apartments of the ladies of the court. They are all reclining on soft cushions. Their curiously carved fans no longer move, and their eyes are earnestly fixed upon seven small pieces of ivory lying before them. Any of the beautiful females in the kingdom would willingly be the wife of Hang-Ho. He is so agreeable, and besides, it would be such a novel way of winning a husband, by finding out a puzzle which even the Emperor could not discover.

The pretty Yang-te-Se is now deeply occupied with the " Puzzle." She is seated at a small table, in her own room, her cheeks are flushed with excitement, and her heart is beating violently, for the poor maiden has suffered much since her lover was condemned to die ; and now, if she does not discover the answer to the puzzle, he is, indeed, lost to her for ever. She presses her hands to her face, and the pearly tears filling her eyes, find their way through those delicate fingers.

Suddenly she hears a slight rustling in the tree that grows beneath her window, and, in an instant, there is nestling in her bosom a beautiful white pigeon.

" Oh, sweet bird," she exclaims, as she kisses it and smooths its feathers, " what bringest thou to me from Hang-Ho ?" Whilst uttering these words, she unties a white ribbon from its neck, attached to which is a small scroll. She unrolls it—glances earnestly at it—and, oh ! it is the key to the puzzle —Hang-Ho is her's !

There is great excitement through the court of the Emperor Ching, for his own daughter has discovered the puzzle. And all the people bow their heads reverently, saying, " Changti certainly watches over the sweet maiden ! Hang-Ho has a nice little wife."

Such is the origin of the " Great Chinese Puzzle."

THE PERILS OF FISHING.

UNDER the shadow of old Monadnock I did all the fishing of my juvenile days. A brighter or a livelier stream never flashed down the side of a rugged mountain, than that which washed the eastern margin of our old homestead farm. Never did prettier, gayer, more bewitching little shiners dance and shimmer in the limpid waters, than those which found a home in that same laughing mountain brook. It sometimes hurt my feelings sadly to see them writhing and wriggling on the hook, or flapping about on the grass, in the agonies of death, and I thought I would rather lose my breakfast than torture them so again. But then again, the roguish little elves would vex me, and try my patience marvelously, till my sympathy with suffering quite evaporated. When I was in the greatest hurry, they would always tease me most. They would actually seem to laugh at my impatience. I could see every rascal of them in the clear, crystal element. They would come dancing gayly up to the hook, smell daintily at the bait,

turn up an eye at me with a most provoking smile, as if to say, "We know too much for that, boy," and then skip away with a titter that I could almost hear. Then up, and away again. Then nibble, nibble, nibble — jerk! and out would come bait, hook, and sinker, but no fish, disturbing the water and frightening away the whole troup, so that it was five minutes, or more, before the boldest of them would venture to come back. Then, try it again, impatiently. Vexation would make me hungry, and the hungry stomach would get the better of the tender heart, and make me resolve to pay the little imps tenfold for their impudence and coquetry. Then, nibble again, nibble—jerk, so impatiently and nervously, that the excited sinker would perhaps give me a hard slap on the nose, and the agitated hook jump into my cheek or hand, and make me scream out with pain and rage.

Many, I assure you, are the perils of fishing, even in a quiet brook. I once had my cheek so torn by the hook, which caught the infection of my passionate jerk, that it was nearly a month before I could remove the patch, and the scar remained a full month or more after that.

Do you see that cosy old fellow, sitting on the arch of the bridge, yonder, the image of patience and laziness. Under the shade of the overhanging trees, and in social chat with his friend, he seems to have a very good time of it, just now. But, by-and-by, when his friend passes on, and he is left alone, perhaps an hour or two, with no occupation

or amusement, but just to hold that line, and look at the water, it will not be quite so interesting, and it may be somewhat dangerous, unless he happens to be a good swimmer.

I know just what it is, for I have experienced it. I was sitting, one bright morning, on a projecting log. that overhung a deep eddy at an angle of the brook, stupidly waiting for the nibbles. The fishes were either very sleepy, or not very hungry, and would not come to my bait. The brook was a little swollen with recent rains, and the whirling eddies were more active and brilliant than usual. I partially forgot my breakfast, and went off into a revery, into which those whirling eddies wove and intertwined themselves till my head was all in a whirl too, and pop! I went into the water. I awoke from my revery in an instant. I knew at once where I was, though sorely puzzled to know why and how I got there. Without stopping to solve that riddle, I dashed and spluttered about, shouting lustily for help, and reducing to instant practice all my knowledge of the art of swimming. I soon reached the bank, but it was loose and slippery, and I could get no hold by which to draw myself up. I shouted again, Help! Help! and soon heard the welcome answer—*Where? what?* hallo! The next minute, my cousin John came rushing to the spot. He had been fishing in the same stream a little above. A large rock projecting from the bank had prevented us from seeing each other. Seeing my trouble, he tore a rail from the fence near by, passed one end of it to me, and by that means drew me around to the spot where he had been sitting, and where the bank was easier to climb. By the help of the rail and John's encouraging words, I was soon on shore and on my way home. I had lost my line, my basket, and my

:ap, and was thoroughly drenched and cold. But,
would you believe it, grateful as I thought I was to
have escaped with my life, I was more annoyed by
the croakings of a poor innocent bull-frog than by
all the other inconveniences and discomforts I experienced. Squatting on the edge of the little pool,
just within the fence, the frog puffed out his cheeks,
and eyed me with a look of contempt, at the same
time saying—pod-dook ! pod-dook ! which I inter-

preted—*poor* **duck***!* **pcor duck***!* I took up a stone
to demolish him, whereupon he plunged into the
pool and was lost to sight for a moment, then, pop-
ping up on the other side, he shouted *pod-dook! pod-
dook!* as lustily as ever. I looked for another
stone, but John laughed at my folly and told me I
had better leave the poor frog to sing out his song,
and hurry home for a change of clothes and a warm
dinner.

But I never hear that "plump, dump," hoarse
song of the bull-frog without something of that old
feeling of rage. If I only could understand what
the dumpy old rascals would say, I should not care.
I have tried in vain to get this song interpreted.
There are as many versions as writers. My father
used to tell a story of "Old Grimes," as he was
called, who, going home one dark night, drunk as a
beast, and passing a pool, heard a hoarse voice say,
"Old Grimes! old Grimes!" Then another answered, "He's a rogue! he's a rogue!" Soon a
chorus broke out, "Let's kill him!" let's kill him!"
and then, with a deep sort of groan, "Get a club!
get a club!" and Grimes hurried home almost
sobered with fright.

There was a famous society, in one of the New
England States, called "The Pahh Duqhh Society,"
a name derived from the solemn utterance of the
frogs, who inhabited a pond near the place where
tho meetings of the society were held. The names
of the officers were all in the same queer froggish

style of spelling, and the advertisements of the meeting and doings, which appeared from time to time in the papers, excited a great deal of wonder among the young folks, But even the learned society did not seem to get any more insight into the meaning of the song than they did into the spelling of the sound.

MY HOME.

THE home I sigh for is no kindred dwelling
　Where eager eyes look wistfully for me,
Where hand meets hand, and hearts with rapture swelling
　Bid the long parted the most loved one be.

Home! smiling home! the lines are o'er it drooping;
　Yet from its chambers children stand aloof;
So low it lies, that thy kind hand in stooping
　Alone may touch its green and humble roof.

Home! peaceful home! the grass doth grow around it;
　For garden flowers the daisies blossom fair;
Narrow its walls—an arm's breadth well may bound i'
　But sound of scorn or wrong can reach not there.

O welcome home! the exile, gazing blindly
　Through tears of tenderness the loved to see,
Haileth his native shore with thoughts less kindly
　Than my poor heart looks hopefully to thee!

There in the dust shall perish Life's last anguish,
　While the freed Soul the purer realms shall soar
Exile no longer from its home to languish,
　And Home!—my Home!—is mine for evermore!

TO-DAY.

　Don't tell me of to-morrow;
　　Give me the man who'll say
　That when a good deed's to be done,
　　Let's do the deed to day!
　We may command the present,
　　If we act and never wait;
　But repentance is the phantom
　　Of the past, that comes too late!

LEAP FROG.

THIS is a most excellent pastime. It should be played in a spacious place, out of doors if possible, and the more they are engaged in it, provided they be of the same height and agility, the better is the sport. We will suppose a dozen at play :—Let eleven of them stand in a row, about six yards apart, with all their faces in one direction, arms folded, or their hands resting on their thighs, their elbows in, and their heads bent forward, so that the chin of each rests on his breast, the right foot advanced, the back a little bent, the shoulders rounded, and the body firm. The last begins the sport by taking a short run, placing his hands on the

shoulders of the nearest player, and leaping with
their assistance—of course, springing with his feet
at the same time—over his head, as represented in
the cut. Having cleared the first, he goes on to the
second, third, fourth, fifth, etc. in succession, and as
speedily as possible. When he has gone over the
last, he goes to the proper distance, and places himself in a position for all the players to leap over
him in their turn. The first over whom he passed,
follows him over the second, third, fourth, etc.; and
when he has gone over, the one who begun the
game places himself in like manner for the others to
jump over him. The third follows the second, and
so on until the parties are tired.

The manner of playing Leap-Frog about London
is different, and, as we think, much inferior in
safety, appearance, and amusement :—A lad places
himself with his hands on his knees, his body nearly
doubled, and his side, instead of his back, turned
toward the leapers, who, with a short run, take
their leap at some distance from the lad who is to be
vaulted over ; he who takes his leap the farthest off,
is reckoned the best player. This, it may be readily imagined, is by no means so lively as the real
game of Leap-Frog, which we have above described.
The boy, who is to be leaped over, receives the
greater shock from the jumpers ; and he is in more
danger of being thrown down by, or having a blow
on his head from, their knees.

THE BUTTERFLY.

" Don't kill me,"—caterpillar said,
　As Clara raised her heel,
Upon the humble worm to tread,
　As though it could not feel.

" Don't kill me,—I will crawl away,
　" And hide away from sight,
" And when I come, some other day,
　" You'll view me with delight,"

The caterpillar went and hid
　In some dark, quiet place,
Where none could look on what he did,
　To change his form and face.

And then, one day, as Clara read
  Within a shady nook,
A butterfly, superbly dressed,
  Alighted on her book.

His shining wings were dotted o'er
  With gold and blue and green,
And Clara owned she naught before
  So beautiful had seen.

"THERE IS A SILVER LINING TO EVERY CLOUD."

THOUGH dark seems the future, and the present is dreary
  Keep still a brave heart and a resolute will ;
In the good cause of progress, oh ! never be weary,
  But fight 'gainst oppression and tyranny still.
Remember, though dark is the cloud that's above you
  And no dazzling sun in the horizon is shining,
And no one in the wide world to care for and love you,
  That to every dark cloud there's a bright silver lining.

Still keep on your way, and your duty pursuing,
  Till your life and your labor and duties are o'er ;
Then receive your reward for your faithful well-doing,
  And fear not oppression or poverty more.
But remember through life, though the voyage be hard,
  For 'twill save thee regret and much sorrowful pining,
Though your stay upon earth has been checkered and barred,
  That to every dark cloud there's a bright silver lining.

HARRY KNOW-NOTHING;

OR, WHICH END WILL YOU HAVE?

HARRY was a genuine know-nothing — not such an one as we have about now-a-days, who profess great love for their country, but show only love to themselves; who know nothing of the true interests of their country, but know enough of other things to be able to do a vast deal of mischief. Harry was a real bona-fide know-nothing—an ignoramus, who loved play, and hated work, who loved idleness, and hated books, and who, consequently, never learned anything useful, or failed to learn anything mischievous. His mother was very indulgent, and gave him a great variety of playthings, seeming to have no other wish than that Harry should " enjoy himself." His father did not quite approve this kind of education, and used often to say, that, if Harry did not soon alter his course, and learn something useful, he would certainly " come out of the little end of the horn " at last.

When Harry was a very little boy, he had a kite

given him, which was taller than he was himself. He did not know how to manage it, and would not wait till his father came home, to show him. He rushed out. at once, into the road. His mother followed with little Charley, and offered her assistance. But Harry, as know-nothings generally do, thought he knew all about the matter. He laid the kite down on the ground, and then, unrolling his string, ran furiously off, without heeding which way the wind was blowing. As might be expected, he ran the wrong way. The kite did not rise, but was dragged along in the dust, till it encountered a stone, and then, snap went the back-bone, and the kite was spoiled. Harry took up the wreck, found the paper torn in several places, and the whole toy utterly past mending. At this he cried violently, and blamed his mother, for not preventing it. And then—for thoughtless boys are always unreasonable —he fell into a passion with Charley, because he laughed, and said " Mamma good—Harry naughty." Just then, Harry's father came along, and, when he

saw how things were going, he took Harry into the
house, and had a long talk with him, trying to show
the folly of passion, and the evils of idleness.
"Harry, my dear," said he, "if you do not improve,
you will surely come out of the little end of the
horn."

As Harry grew older, he only grew more fond of
play, and more in love with idleness and mischief.
When he was ten years old, he could not read
respectably, and could not write a word, or a letter.
He had been sent to school, but gave no attention
to his lessons. He often strayed away into the
fields, or stopped by the way, to play with all the idle
boys he met. Many a time, I have seen him in the

road, his cap thrown carelessly on the ground, and
his satchel by its side, wasting half the morning in
playing at ball, or marbles, with some companion as
himself, and paying no heed to the call of the bell,
when it rang the hour for school to open. Harry
thought this was all fun, and that he knew the way

to be happy, better than father, or mother, or teacher, or all the world beside.

Well, in time Harry became a man. His father died. His mother was poor and he was compelled to do something for his own living. But what could he do. He had never learned anything useful. He had no habits of study, or application, or self-denial, all of which are essential to any kind of success. Nobody had confidence enough in him, to trust him with any important matter, or regard enough for him, to make any great effort to help him. He tried various kinds of occupation, but proved so ignorant and unskillful in all that he undertook to do, that nobody was willing to employ him long. The employment he obtained was of the lowest and most laborious kind, and that which brought the poorest wages. Harry was often tired and often hungry. He frequently regretted the idle and unprofitable course he had pursued, and wished he had given heed to the advice of his father. Had he been a good reader and writer, with habits of diligence, he might have secured a clerkship in some mercantile house, or a place in a railroad office. Had he given early attention to his arithmetic, he might have become an engineer, or a surveyor, or perhaps a teacher. But, alas! poor Harry, he was fit for nothing, but plain hard work. He had no resources in himself—no knowledge of history, or the world, no thoughts worth dwelling upon. And, when he thought of his early home, of his kind father, of the

many lessons he had received, the warnings he had
wantonly slighted, he felt and acknowledged that
he was already, as his father had often predicted,
coming out of the

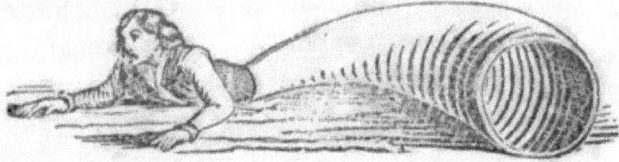

LITTLE END OF THE HORN.

A GOOD RULE.—It is always a good rule to follow, to step in no path, to speak no word, to commit no act, when conscience appears to whisper,
Beware. You had better wait a twelvemonth, and
learn your duty, than to take a hasty step, and
bring tears and repentance to a dying day. How
many a lost man might have been saved, had he listened to an inward monitor, and resisted the first
inclination to deviate from the holy path of recti-
tude. See far away before you, and on either side,
the ground whitened with the bones and sinews of
millions who have perished ignobly in the march of
life. They resisted the spirit of truth, and fell.
They trusted to themselves, and sunk at the onset.
Take warning by them." Could their bones live,
breathe, and speak, how earnestly would they appeal to you! They would compel you, as it were,
to pursue a virtuous course, that your end might be
joyous and not degraded.

THE CHILD AND THE ANGEL.

"Alone upon the beach I stray,
The curling waves around me play
I sing my merry roundelay,"
    Thus spake a little child.
" Sweet child," said I, " why free from care,
Why stray you fearless everywhere,
Nor have a thought of how you'll fare
    When storms are howling wild?"

" Once on a time, I dreamed a dream,
And, stranger, then it seemed to seem
As though an angel's kindly beam
    Shone, dazzling, round my head.
That beauteous form, it said to me,
' I shall thy guardian angel be ;
Therefore be fearless, wild, and free,
    Nor make thy cares like lead.

" ' When future cares before thee rise,
Think not of them, but be thou wise ;
Seize every moment as it flies,
    And do thy duty then.
Thus shalt thou do that which is right,
Which having done with heart contrite,
When Death removes, thou't live in light,
    Far, far from human ken.'

" Thus spake the angel unto me,
And this is why I'm merry, free,
Gladsome, blithe, and full of glee—
    I do my duty now."
"Yes, child, thour't right, thou doest well,
Thy seniors thou dost much excel ;
I'll go and thy sweet lesson tell
    To every one I know."

STORY OF THE TWO MILLERS,
OR THE DANGER OF DELAY.

JOHN and William Davis were millers, and occupied a place on the side of the river. A channel
which had been cut from the river supplied them
with water, and no one ever passed the little foot-
bridge, by the flood-gates, without peeping into the
mill ; for the hoppers made such a clatter, and the
socks went up and down so briskly, that it was
quite clear John and William Davis were doing
considerable business. Up in the morning at five,
they industriously began the busy day, and it was
only when the river was very low that the water-
wheels were not whirling round amid the foaming
waters.

The mill had belonged to their father before them, and had got much out of repair ; and the roof let in the rain, and the river had, by little and little, worn away the bank till there was some fear that the foundation of the mill would be weakened. John and William were told this by their neighbors—they saw it with their own eyes ; but still they delayed repairing the roof and the embankment, till the danger had considerably increased. " We must do something to them next summer," said John. " Ay," replied William, " for if we do not, the mill will come down sure enough." The summer came, but as it was not a very dry one, they continued very busy, and the repairs of the mill were quite out of the question. " I tell you what," said William, " it does not signify talking, but the mill must be repaired this next summer." " True," replied John, " for if it be not, we shall soon have it about our ears." Notwithstanding these resolutions, summer came and went, and no repairs took place at the mill.

Now all this time, the rain was pelting worse and worse through the roof, and the bank was being washed away by little and little, till every neighbor saw that the danger was great. John and William had, from time to time, patched up, here and there, a hole in the roof, and now and then put a few spades of earth against the bank, but all this amounted to nothing. Indeed it was worse than nothing, for it only deceived them into a belief of their security.

"I am thinking," said Mr. Horton, the stone-mason, as he passed one windy day over the foot-bridge, "that neither this bridge nor the mill will stand fifty years longer. The first flood will bring an old house over somebody's head."

Mr. Horton saw the danger but too clearly, for that very same day the river rose rapidly, in conse-quence of the rain which had fallen on the hills, and the wind and rain beat upon the roof of the mill till a part of it fell in with a terrible crash. This was a sad affair, for now there was no possibility of putting off the repairs, though it was a bad time of the year to begin them. John and William went off in a hurry to consult Mr. Horton about the expense of a new roof, but while they were talking about it, Samuel Ball, the miller's man, came breathless with haste, and pale with fear, to tell them that the river had undermined the foundation of the mill, and that one-half of it was level with the ground.

John and William Davis had been recommended, fifty times over, to build a new mill a little further from the running waters, but they thought of the ex-pense, and hoped the old mill would last at least a few years longer, especially as every summer they intended to put it in repair. They had, however, neglected to repair the old mill, and delayed to build a new one, till it was too late. The old one was now in a condition too bad to be repaired, and they had no new one to remove to. So they lost at once, their mill, their customers, and their means of

TIMOTHY FENNEL'S REFLECTIONS

EVERY body knows that Timothy's mother was a very "reflecting" woman. When Timothy proposed a visit to New York, the old lady would only consent to his entering so wicked a place on condition that he should make "practical reflections" on all that he saw. So he came to our city, and saw everything that was visible, but forgot all about the moral reflections, until the time had nearly come for him to return home. He now began to reflect on the reflections his mother would cast upon him, when she knew how unreflecting he had been. However, he resolved to make the most of what time remained; so, having seated himself in a Broadway stage, he mused somewhat in the following manner:

"Shakspeare said that 'all the world is a stage.' Now if the world is a stage, a stage is all the world. Nothing is more evident. Now, I'll see what the resemblances are, and here is one, right at hand. Before I entered this stage it was empty—not a single occupant. So it once was with this world—both nicely fitted up for man, but as yet no man to occupy them, and then Adam took posses-

sion of the world, and so have I of this stage.
Striking comparison! I feel Adam to be a brother.
Wonder if he didn't feel lonely? I do. Wonder
if he didn't feel it was a pity that so much room
should be wasted? I do. Yes, Adam, you and I
have a common bond of sympathy! But here comes
a woman, another Eve. Resemblance holds good,
all but the Eden, for I must confess I don't find
that quiet repose which I imagine them to have enjoyed. *This* road is rough, but it probably refers
to the world after the fall. There the analogy will
hold again. Life is rough, to be sure, a stony
ground, and we are whirled over it with little regard to our individual feelings. Think a few more
inhabitants here would give some stability to our
movements—and we shall have them no doubt, for
the world soon began to be filled. And, sure enough,
here comes a Cain, and an Abel, a Seth and Enos,
and still they come, men, women, and children.

Now we are full—rather more crowded than the
people of the world are. We jog on together, knowing little of each other, caring less. Still a resemblance. Well, what a variety of forms, faces, and
manners! Analogy good. Here's a man who
evidently feels that he has the undisputed right to
as much space as any other two persons. Esquire
Thorne, of our place. And there are these same
Esquire Thornes in every place, And there is a
little woman who has shrunk back into herself, until she seems to occupy no space at all ; she is wil-

ling to yield her rights to such a big man as Esquire
Thorne. One of the Aunt Marys of the world.
There is a youth who is evidently making a great
effort to extend himself to such proportions as
would suit the dignity of a full-grown man. Shakspeare *was* a wise man! A child cries—just as it
should be! What would this world be without
cries and tears? And here is another resemblance.
We have nothing to do in guiding this vehicle.
The reins are in the hands of another, and we are,
for the time being, entirely at his disposal; so
there's One who guides the affairs of this world, in-
dependently of any acts of ours. Mother will like
that thought, I am sure. But lo! one has come to
his destination. So man has an appointed time on
the earth, and the end will come—to some the road
is longer, but every road has an end. He pays the
debt of nature (in the form of a sixpence), and is
gone. There is a vacant seat, but here comes some
one to fill it. "One generation passeth away, and
another cometh." Analogy perfect. And now our
new-comer sits there just as if he had had the earli-
est and sole title, and even we have almost forgotten the face of the first occupant. The world
exactly! Only a few weeks ago Dr. Maghtean died,
and we all mourned, and said a man could never be
found to fill his place, his death had made such a
breach. Now Dr. Bardow is carrying his saddle-
bags, and half the people have forgotten that it was
not always Dr. Bardow, and they are just as will-

ing to take their certificate for leaving the world
from Dr. Bardow as from Dr. Maghtean ; and Dr.
Bardow has forgotten, too, and thinks no more of
those who were before him, or who shall be after
him, than does the present subject of our reflections.
And now they are dropping off, one by one. So
goes the world, "Friend after friend departs," and
if I don't depart soon from this stage, I shall be
left the sole occupant again. Sure enough! I am
all alone. Hope I shall not be left the last one in
this world, for, as Jenny Lind said, "who would
inhabit this world alone?" Hope at any rate my
mother will stay and live with me. That will be
a pleasing reflection for mother. I'll lay stress
on that, for I shall wish to come to New York
again. Stage stops. Well, I suppose I may say
I've passed through the world, and the time of my
departure is at hand, and I feel entirely ready to
leave this moving scene. Hope I may be as willing
to leave the world when my time comes. Poor, old
stage, you will not always last. I see signs of de-
cay even now, and I suppose the time will come
when you will be good for nothing but fuel for the
fire, and, so, as my good mother often remarks, this
world is to be burned up at some future day. Oh !
Shakspeare was a wise man. "This world is a
stage," and a stage is this world.

THE PLOUGH BOY.

WHERE winds blow pure and freely,
 And blossoms load the air,
And green trees wave their leafy boughs,
 And all around looks fair,
I ply my daily labor,
 And work till night has come ;
And then return contented,
 To rest myself at home.

How sweet unto the weary,
 Is such unvexed repose,
When evening's length'ning shadows
 Around our cottage close ;
And with quiet in our bosoms,
 We sit in twilight's shades,
And watch the crimson radiance,
 As from the west it fades.

And then how fresh the slumber,
    Which falls upon our eyes ;
When night's clear dews are falling,
    And stars are in the skies !
No feverish dreams affright us,
    And make us start, and weep ;
But trusting in God's kindly care,
    We kindly sink to sleep.

And then ere morning flushes
    Along the eastern skies,
We bless the care that watched us,
    And, nerved to labor, rise.
We see the day-star fading,
    We see the vapors glide,
Along the misty vales below
    And up the mountain's side.

Again our hardy sinews
    Are bent to manly toil,
Again we mow the waving grass,
    Or plough the dewy soil.
And ever when our labors
    For the day are past and done,
We sit before our cottage door,
    And watch the setting sun.

———— •♦• ————

Sown in darkness, or sown in light,
Sown in weakness, or sown in might,
Sown in meekness, or sown in wrath,
 n the broad world-field or the shadowy path,
            Sure will the harvest be.

SPELLING THE DICTIONARY.

ROWNJOHN, our teacher who wielded the hickory sceptre a while in the old brown school-house on the corner, where the rudiments of learning were worked into my head, had a daily exercise in spelling somewhat out of the common course. Each member of our class selected from the dictionary any word he pleased, taking care to learn both how to spell it and how to define it. At the close of the ordinary spelling-lesson, the scholar who stood at the head of the class spelled the word he had selected, and then the next below gave the definition of it, if he could. If he could not, the word was passed down farther, till it came to some one able to tell its meaning. Whoever did this took his place in the class above as many as had failed. Then the second from the head spelled his word, and the definition of it was called for along down the line in a similar manner. And so on till all had given out their selections.

That was not a bad plan, was it? Many a worse thing may be done in school than learning the dictionary. Have you never heard how Daniel

Webster answered one who inquired in what way
he could become skillful and fluent in the use of
language? "Read dictionaries," said he; "I read
dictionaries. Are such books too dry to read,
think you? There is great benefit in reading them,
nevertheless; I know that from my own experience. Anybody might know as much from his
own common sense. Why, just think a minute. A
good English Dictionary, for instance, contains all
the words in our language, together with an exhibition of their meaning and use. What readier
way, then, can one take, to form an acquaintance
with our language, and to gain a full command of
it, than to study the dictionary, and transfer its
treasures to the mind?

THE SCHOOLBOYS.

This, though, is not what I set out to say, exactly. I had in mind, a little incident connected with our spelling and defining, that amused us prodigiously one day. A certain scholar, remarkable for nothing in particular, except for a quantity of sense a little less than common, when his turn came to deliver the word he had selected, roared out with considerable vigor, *"b-u-t, but."* Instantly we all put on a broad grin, and turned our eyes to the teacher to see what turn affairs would take. We had to wait but a short time for that. Mr. Brownjohn soon began, as usual, to call for the definition of the word. I suspect he did so just for form's sake. If he really thought we could give the meaning of such a word as *but*, he must have had a pretty high opinion of our abilities, or, at least, of our acquaintance with the niceties of language. Had we thought of it, we might, indeed, have referred to Noah Webster's famous old spelling-book, where, next to " *butt*, a barrel," stood " *but*, except." In fact, however, none of us thought of it ; nor would that account of the matter have thrown much light into our minds, had some one chanced to have refreshed our memories with it.

Down went the word along the class, one frankly owning that he could tell nothing about it, and another shaking his head in sign of ignorance ; till at length a fellow who stood away toward the foot, began to show symptoms of having caught the idea. His eye twinkled, a smile of satisfaction beamed in his face, and he stood with one foot advanced, ready for a movement along up the line. His whole look and manner thus declared to us, about as plainly as his tongue could, " Ah! now I have it." He seemed impatient to deliver himself, and the instant his turn came he sounded out boldly —" *but end of a log ;*" and before the word was fairly out of his mouth, he made a spring for a considerably higher place in the class. Mr. Brownjohn gave him a check, however, and told him that his definition of the word would hardly do. If we had not then a hearty laugh all round, then we never had one in that old brown school-house.

" Did not that fellow pass among his companions for a genius?" I rather think not. I never heard anything of the kind. If I remember right, we considered him remarkable for nothing but this : he had a way, both in speaking and in reading, of putting what we called a *hook* on to the end of a word ; as, for example, " All men think all men mortal but themselves—eh." It may be, though, that he had genius, and that it began to bud on that very day when that little incident happened. At any rate, I know that he grew to something afterward. Only three or four of those who attended our school at that time ever got a liberal education ; and he was one of them.

After leaving college, he worked himself up in the world to—I can't tell you where. The last time I heard of him, which was several years ago,

he was laboring as a teacher in a high-school. You
see there is no telling beforehand what a boy will
make. Sometimes dull scholars, and those who are
despised and laughed at, yet wake up and outstrip
their fellows, and come to shine as lights in the
world.

ON A GOOD HOUSE-DOG CALLED "WATCH."

Poor faithful Watch ! thy watch of life is o'er,
And mute and senseless near the kitchen door
Thou layest, a breathless corpse, where thou stood to guard
    before ;
Thy pliant temper, known and praised by all,
Thy prompt obedience to thy master's call ;
Whether to climb the hill, or scour the plain,
Or drive enroaching hogs from out the lane ;
Thy quick return, on motion of his hand,
To guard the door, or wait a fresh command ;
Thy joy to meet at eve, with fawning play,
Domestic faces, absent but a day ;
Thy bark, that might the boldest thief affright,
And patient watch, through many a dreary night—
All speak thy worth, but none could save thy breath,
For what is merit 'gainst the shafts of death ;
Sleep, then, my dog ! thy tour of duty o'er,
Where thief and trav'ler can disturb no more ;
Content t' have gained all that thou canst have—
Thy master's plaudit, and a peaceful grave !

OLD WHITTEMORE HILL.

FEW there are among our readers but that the recollection of some old hill, or stream, or glen, wakes in their hearts, the memories of early childhood, and recalls to mind the scenes of youthful days of pleasure and of joy.   To me the old Whittemore hill—with its stately pine on its very summit with solemn look toward heaven, though blasted by the lightning's flash, and stripped of all its early green—stands as a beacon light between childhood and old age, reminding me that men— like trees—grow old, and die ; and yet bringing back the loved scenes of early youth with all their joys and happiness, making every pulse beat with fresh vigor, and I feel as young as when, on the first fourth of July I was large enough for my mother

to think it prudent for me to undertake the difficult
task of trying to ascend to the top without assistance. I made the effort ; the result was a decided
success. Standing on the top-most stone, the proud-
est day of my life—for though I have ascended many
times since to a far greater height, yet never with
such wild enthusiasm and bursting joy—I shouted
and hallooed to the extent of my lungs till woodland and vale, and the surrounding hills echoed
back the "sounding joy." And then the sight
that met my view. At the foot of the hill, the old
Souhegan river meandered through the meadows in
slow and solemn flow towards the ocean. Large
tracts of woodland—wide spreading vales—thriving villages, and long line of mountains were
spread out before me in all their beauty. I supposed the whole world was then visible before me,
I fancied that old "Watatic" was Mt. Vesuvius,
and wondered why the crater did not burn. To
the west, the "Rocky Mountains," were plainly visible, while to the north and east the "Himalays"
and "Mountains of the Moon" rose "highest in
the world." "Wachuset," to the south was the
commencement of the range of the "Andes," while
far to the west, beyond all others rose grand "Mo-
nadnoc"—the "Chimborazo" of my geography—
"five miles high above the level of the sea,"—said
geography being whipped into me by old Birch, who
ruled supreme in the square-roofed school-house at
the foot of the Hill, upon which I now looked down

THE NOISY CHILDREN JUST LET LOOSE FROM SCHOOL.

with contempt. Not but that I enjoyed going to
school as much as any one, for I could play as hard
and as long as any of them when let loose from school,
and as I look back to those early days I can only
wish that the hours of study had been better spent,
that the hours of play could have been better enjoyed. Don't try to get through school too fast,
boys, or finish your studies too quick. I was
ready to take the burden old Father Time had for

me to bear, before I knew its weight, or was prepared to battle with the stern duties of life. You
will find as I did, that you could not see all the
world at once from the top of one little hill, however high, and however much loved ; be patient, act
well your part each day, as the day comes round,
and let night find each duty done, then, with light
hearts of joy, lie down to pleasant dreams.

"AN AX TO GRIND."

ORIGIN OF THE TERM.

WHEN I was a little boy, says Dr. Franklin, I remember one cold winter morning I was accosted by a smiling man with an ax on his shoulder. "My pretty boy," said he, "has your father a grindstone ?" "Yes, sir," said I. "You are a fine little fellow, said he ; "will you let me grind my ax on it ?" Pleased with the compliment of the "fine little fellow," "O yes," I answered ; "it is down in the shop." "And will you, my little fellow," said he, patting me on the head, "get me a little hot water ?" Could I refuse? I ran and soon brought a kettle full. "How old are you and what's your name ?" continued he, without waiting for a reply ; "I am sure you are one of the finest little fellows that I ever saw—will you just turn a few minutes for me ?" Tickled at the flattery, like a fool I went to work, and bitterly did I rue the day. It was a new ax, and I toiled and tugged till I was almost tired to death. The school-bell rang and I could not get away ; my hands were blistered, the ax was sharpened, and the man turned to me with, "Now, you little rascal, you've played truant ; scud for school or you'll rue it," Alas ! thought I, it is hard enough to turn the grindstone this cold day, but to be called a little rascal was too much. It sunk deep in my mind, and often have I thought of it since. When I see a merchant over polite to his customers, begging them to take a little brandy, and throwing his goods on the counter, thinks I, that man has an ax to grind. When I see a man flattering the people, making great profession of attachment to liberty, who is in private life a tyrant, methinks, look out, good people, that fellow would set you turning a grindstone. When I see a man hoisted into office by party spirit, without a single qualification to render him respectable or useful, alas! deluded people, you are doomed for a season to turn the grindstone for a body.

SCENE IN A COUNTRY SCHOOL-HOUSE.

"THOMAS, open that door," said the teacher, as a loud pounding was heard in the entry.

Thomas did so, and ushered in three as ragged specimens of humanity as could be found.

"Well, my little man," said the teacher, "what's your name?"

"My name," replied he, "is Dan."

"You mean *Daniel*, said he, raising up his eye brows.

"Yours?" pointing to the next.

"Mine is Sam."

"*Samuel* you mean," said he, with a half smile.

Then, turning to the youngest, he was about to put the same question. But before the words could escape from his mouth, with a grin of triumph the youngster exclaimed, "*Jimuel*."

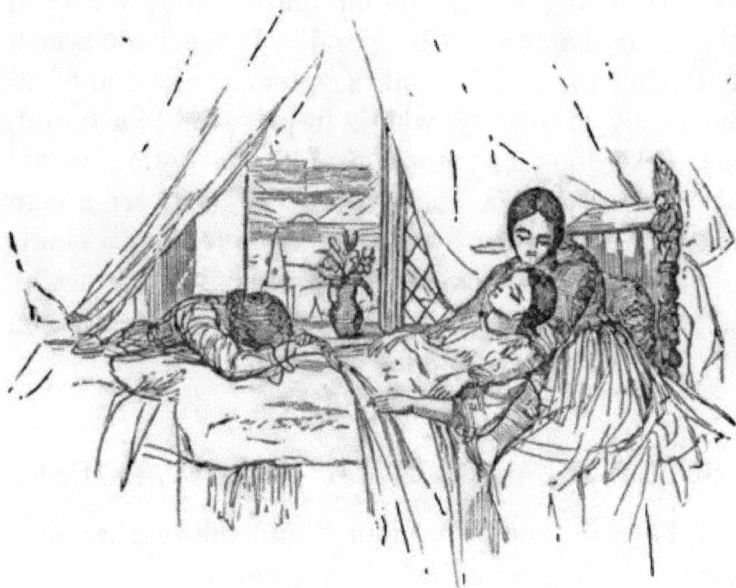

SWEET WILL BE OUR REST.

CHILD ! the day is fleeting past,
   And the night will soon be here,
When to thee I shall be borne
   Slowly on my funeral bier.

Then, my darling, by thy side
   I will lay me down to sleep ;
All my longings will be hushed,
   While dear ones above us weep.

And within this lowly bed,
   Father, brother, sister dear—
All the loved ones of thy heart
   Soon shall be beside thee here.

'Neath the mantle of the grave,
　Slumbering on earth's quiet breast
Till the morning light shall dawn,
　Sweet, my child, will be our rest.

May we wake, on that bright morn,
　With a sin-forgiven heart—
Meet around the great white Throne
　Never, never more to part.

LOOK AT HOME.

SHOULD you feel inclined to censure
　Faults which you in others view,
Ask your own heart ere you venture,
　If that has not failings too.

Let not friendly vows be broken—
　Rather strive a friend to gain ·
Many a word in anger spoken
　Finds its passage home again.

Do not, then, in idle pleasure,
　Trifle with a brother's fame ;
Guard it as a sacred treasure,
　Sacred as your own good name.

Do not form opinions blindly—
　Hastiness to trouble tends ;
hose of whom we've thought unkindly,
　Oft become our warmest friends.

THE PRACTICAL JOKER.

ARTHUR M—— was a bright little boy of ten years, and his pleasant face and cheerful spirit seemed like a ray of heaven's own blessed sunlight in his mother's otherwise solitary dwelling. But I am sorry to say Arthur was not loved by his companions. He was a practical joker, and his little friends were in constant fear, when in his company, of having some very unpleasant trick played upon them. If they went to gather nuts or berries, he did love to kill a snake and throw it around some boy's neck, just for the fun of hearing him scream. When they went to bathe, they often found a frog in their pockets, or their shoes would be filled with angle worms. And he was sometimes so very cruel as to take away a boy's dinner, and fill his basket with stones.

These things were very annoying, and at length Arthur was left to play alone, or to go home to his little sister. Dear little Eliza was just beginning to go to school, and Arthur loved her very much. But his love of fun, as he called it, was sometimes so strong, that he would even overturn his sled, and throw the sweet little girl into the snow. His mother strove in vain to correct this cruel propensity, and she felt some anxiety on his account when a new father came to take charge of his education. His own father died when he was a babe, and of course he had never known a father's love. But he was very much pleased when a pleasant, smiling gentleman came to live with them, and he was told he might call him father.

One morning, a few days after Mrs. M——— was married to Mr. L., Arthur was told to cut some potatoes, and give them to the cow. He obeyed very cheerfully, cut the potatoes, and carried them to the barn; but when he placed them before the cow, he turned a peck measure over them, so that the cow could not eat them. "My son,' said Mr. L. when he returned, "did you give the potatoes to the cow?" "Yes sir," he replied, but the merry twinkle of his eye led his father to suspect something wrong, and he very soon went to the barn himself. Arthur was frightened when he saw him go out, for he expected a whipping. But no notice was taken of the *joke*, as he called it,

Soon there was a snow-storm; and when it passsed away, the snow lay piled in drifts on both sides the road. Arthur started for school the next morning, drawing his little sister on his sled; but when he came near the deep drifts, suddenly the sled was overturned, and Eliza was buried in the snow. Arthur sprang to take her up, and very tenderly led her back to the house. But his father stood at the window, and saw the whole transaction. Next morning Mr. L. said pleasantly, "I'll draw you to school this morning, if you like." Arthur was delighted. He thought his father was very kind indeed. But when they came to the drift, suddenly the sled was overturned, and he was buried in the snow.

"You must learn to hold on better than this," said Mr. L. "if you mean I shall draw you." And he quietly returned to the house, leaving Arthur to get out as he could.

"O! chicken for dinner! chicken for dinner! shouted Arthur as he returned from school and saw his favorite dish on the table, They were soon seated, and Mr. L. helped Arthur to a large plate full. But just as he was taking up his knife and fork, his father took up a large bowl that stood by his plate, and turned it over Arthur's dinner. At first he looked in surprise, but he immediately understood it. He was very hungry, but he did not dare to remove the bowl. The rest of the family began to eat, but he sat looking very red and unhappy. At length he burst into tears.

"Father," said he, "I never will put the peck measure over the cow's dinner again, and I'll never turn sissy into the snow again, if you'll let me eat my dinner."

"Very well, my son," said Mr. L., removing the bowl; "you find practical jokes are not very pleasant when played upon yourself. Always remember that if you would be loved and respected, you must do by others as you wish others to do by you."

THE SUNBEAM'S MISSION.

A GENTLE sunbeam lost his way,
In a lonely glen one day,
And rested on a little child,
Whose face was fair, whose eyes were dim
With tears that fell unchecked by him.
And now he speaks in accents wild,
Why am I but an orphan child ?
There once was one who cared for me,
But now she sleeps beneath the tree
A victim to earth's villainy!
But the sunbeam kisses his brow ;
And a smile is on his fair face now.
With face upturned he breathes a prayer
That God will for the orphan care.
And now he leaves that lonely spot,
All care is o'er, all fear forgot,
For now he trusts the orphan's friend,
Whose love and care can never end.
But years have flown on eagle's wings,
And that boy to God still clings ;
And what's the fruit of all his trust ?
And has his hopes been turned to dust ?
Oh ! no, for as a man he stands
Rich and honored by the land ;
And in the busy scene of life,
Where nought is going on but strife,
We see that man stand side by side
With those who are the country's pride.

KINDNESS.

" A WORD fitly spoken, how good is it!" It may for a moment be covered up by the rubbish of worldly care, even as the acorn is by the " dark, damp mould ;" but by-and-by there will be a disturbing of the leaves, and a slender green sprig will spring up " to the sunshine and the dew." So with kindness ; it is never lost. Even the untutored mind of the savage never forgets the cup of cold water given him when in distress.

Be kind! My young friend, give these words deep tracing on your heart's tablet, and let them be ever present with you. Harsh words fall grating on the ear, are poisonous to the heart, and rankle long after the utterer has forgotten them. Even as old letters, when least thought of, arise and add fearfully to the scale in which the actions of the past are to be weighed, so unkind words will instigate and urge onward to revenge. When you are most in need of sympathy from those you have injured, it will be withheld : the fire of your anguish will be to the mirror of memory what heat is to the sheet on which thoughts have been traced in that peculiar ink which needs fire to bring it out to the sight ; your character will be revealed in its true light, your standing on its true basis.

The young should be kind to the aged ! God commands it, conscience reiterates the demand, and, the principle of respect inherent in the bosom of every mortal, urges a compliance ; likewise the thought that in after years the now joyous youth may be subjected to the same treatment by those who have no regard for gray hairs, add its weight in furtherance of the command. "Honor thy father and thy mother" is applicable to all classes ; the amplitude to this commandment, it appears to us, has no latitude shorter than the ends of the earth.

> "Brightest links in life are broken
> By a single angry-word ;"

and a vapor, deadly as the air of the eastern valley, will enshroud in its folds a circle once bound by the sweetest and tenderest ties, but now, by discordant words and harsh expressions, made rancorous and thirsty for revenge.

In heaven there is no discord. How, then, can you expect an entrance into that holy place when your very presence would defile it ?

The air of Pandemonium rings with wailing and bitter reproaches. This, and this only, is the fitting and will be the eternal abode of those who scruple not on earth to destroy unity and sever the tender, vibrating chord of love by harshness and unkind tones.

"Follow me," said the Holy One when on earth ; and as he was "holy, harmless, and undefiled," so we should follow him in this as in other respects. He went about "doing good," and though "reviled,

he reviled not again." Such is the example we
have to follow. Shall we fail? Oh no! Let our
actions ever be kindly ones, and even " as holy oil "
our conversation : "so shall we not fail of our
reward."

THE SIEGE OF BELGRADE.

An Austrian Army, Awfully Arrayed,
Boldly By Battery Besieged Belgrade ;
Cossack Commanders Cannonading Come,
Dealing Destruction's Devastating Doom ;
Every Endeavor Engineers Essay,
For Fame, For Fortune Fighting—Furious Fray ;
Generals 'Gainst Generals Grapple—Gracious God !
How Honors Heav'n Heroic Hardihood !
Infuriate, Indiscriminate, In Ill,
Kinsmen Kill Kindred, Kindred Kinsmen Kill !
Labor Low Levels Longest, Loftiest lines :
Men March 'Mid Mounds, 'Mid Moles, Mid Murd'rous Mines ;
Now Noisy, Noxious Numbers Now Naught
Of Outward Obstacles Opposing Ought ;
Poor Patriots ! Partly Purchas'd, Partly Press'd,
Quite Quaking, Quickly " Quarter, Quarter," Quest,
Reason Returns, Religious Rights Redounds,
Suwarrow Stops Such Sanguinary Sounds ;
Truce To Thee, Turkey ! Triumph To Thy Train !
Unjust, Unwise, Unmerciful Ukraine !
Vanish Vain Victory !—Vanish Victory Vain !
Why Wish we Warfare ?   Wherefore Welcome Were
Xerxes, Ximenes, Xanthus, Xavier ?
Yield, Yield, Ye Youths ! Ye Yoeman, Yield You Yell !
Zeno's Zarpater's Zoroaster's Zeal ;
Attracting All Arms, Against Acts Appeal.

APRIL.

APRIL is a fitful child,
  Full of wayward fancies
Laughing, weeping, sober wild,
Sunny, showery, frantic, mild—
  Anything that chances.

April is a fickle fool,
    Knowing not his season ;
Like a truant out of school.
Out of temper, out of rule,
    Out of rhyme and reason.

April is a mere coquette,
    Ill-behaved in meeting ;
Warm and cool, and dry and wet,
Apt to tantalize and fret—
    Very fond of cheating.

April is a faithless youth,
    Speaks but to undo it ;
Like a broken limb, or tooth,
Trust his honor or his truth,
    And you'll surely rue it.

April is an arrant wag,
    Full of idle humors ;
Apt to grumble, apt to brag,
Sure to give your hopes the bag.
    Ere they come to bloomers.

April will not tend your sheep,
    He will kill or lose them ;
Give him what you will to keep,
He will wake and he will sleep
    Only to abuse them.

What is like an April day,
    Save a broken promise ?
When he sweeps the clouds away,
Smiling softly—who can say
    What of that to come is ?

GUESS WHAT!

THE snow-clouds in the blue sea of heaven had sailed softly out of sight, and the virgin flakes had sunk into the earth. So Mr. E. hastened his preparations, and was soon on his way to another State. As he expected to be absent several days, the house seemed duller in the sunshine than a few hours before, when a storm was apparently gathering. The prospect was rather gloomier than usual, because the children were suffering from colds, and were for the time household prisoners. But, what with reading, winding yarn, swinging in the playroom, and chatting, that day and the next at length came to an end.

It was early dusk, when a startling knock was heard at the front door. "Why don't he ring the bell?" As nobody answered, no one was wiser for the question. Again that knock! The children's curiosity is fairly aroused, and they listen attentively. Soon Bridget ascends the stairs, bringing a nice-looking oblong parcel. Taking it from her, Mrs. E. finds it directed to herself, in an unknown hand. "By Paine's express," reads Louisa alond, peering curiously around the package. "What *can* it be?" exclaims the wondering Ally. "Glass within," "With care," is next discovered upon the wrapper. The children are on tiptoe with expectation. It is evidently a superfine parcel from the city, done up with great care, and forwarded with some urgency. Now, as nothing had been ordered nothing, of course, was expected. Then there was no clue from whom it came, or what it might contain. To be sure, " Glass within" seemed definite enough ; but then, what *kind* of glass? Here was a broad field for speculation. Was it rose or sapphire color ? was it crimson or topaz, emerald or variegated ? Was it in the form of an antique vase, a graceful pitcher, a classic urn, a curious box, or something prettier and more wonderful still? In short, *what was it ?* By this time, the children's imaginations were winged for an airy height. Louise, who is given to castle-building, suggested all sorts of improbable, Aladdin-like marvels. Ally, who is more practical, made rather more substantial guesses, which were fanciful enough.

In the mean time, the parcel, as to its externals, had been thoroughly examined and re-examined. "What do *you* think it is, mother ?" Mrs. E. had no possible data for determining aught but the size and material of the enveloped mystery : but in order to take down the children's high anticipations, she quietly ventured, "A bottle of medicine," heartily joining in the merry laugh her absurd guess excited.

To unloose the mysterious parcel was the only way to satisfy all parties. This Louisa petitioned to do ; but her mother, fearing that in her tremulous excitement she might break or otherwise injure the frail unknown, thought it safest to do it herself. She had early learned a lesson from that admirable story, " Waste not, want not," and almost never *cut* a string. So she cautiously began to untie and unwind. Knot seemed to multiply after knot, and winding to double after winding. Patiently her fingers toiled, and slowly the twine was untied and unwound, and straightened, while three pairs of eyes were steadily watching the process. At length the string was fairly off, and laid aside. Then the brown paper was carefully removed ; but lo! another covering! With how much painstaking had the treasure been inclosed! The second wrapper in its turn was removed ; but still a third guarded the contents. So the six eyes watched on, till the talked about, longed-for mystery stood revealed to their wondering gaze. And what do you *guess* was the great secret ? Will you *give up ?* Well, then, it was neither more nor less than a— bottle of " *Brown's Marsh Mallow,*" " for the cure of colds, coughs, consumptions, bronchial difficulties," and all like *et cetera*—which a careful father had purchased, and left to be directed and forwarded, little dreaming of the wild speculations to which it would give birth, and of the blank dissapointment which would ensue. Shall I pin a moral to the end of my story ? Be moderate in your expectations, and you will be spared many a disappointment.

WINTER.

POOR old hoary winter! How bitterly every body complains of him, and yet how much real fun he brings. See this old man, almost freezing with the cold, hugging his hands, to keep them warm, and wading, almost to the top of his boots, in the wet snow. He grumbles sadly at old Winter, and wishes he would take himself off, as suddenly as he came. He does not seem to know how he shall get along, but he cannot stop, or turn back, and the only way to keep warm, is to keep moving. It is my opinion that, if he had taken nothing but cold water inside, the cold water and snow outside would not make him feel so uncomfortable. Let us follow him a little way, and see how he gets along, and how much good his grumbling does him.

His little dog is ever at his heels, and seems not to be in any great trouble about the snow. He skims over it very easily. He, too, stopped at the tavern, as they came along, but he drank nothing but water. That is one reason why he is so frisky. There, the man has turned the corner, and looks wistfully ahead, to see if there is any comfort in the prospect. It looks gloomy to him, but to those boys yonder, coasting down the hill, on their smooth-shod cutters, it is all bright, cheerful, glorious. He thinks how happy he was once, when as a boy, he revelled in the snow, and flew over the ice on his iron shoes. He wonders that a few years of time should make such a difference. He forgets that some men, older than he, are boys yet, and would take as much pleasure as any of them, in coasting, skating, or sleigh-riding. He dreads water, outside or inside, and the more "fire-water" he takes inside, the more he finds it necessary to hug the stove, to keep his outer man warm. Well, I am sorry for him, and wish he would try the "pledge," and keep it. The pledge, well kept, is as good as a blanket, or a stove, to keep one warm. The pledge, well kept, is a warm coat, a comfortable house, a cheerful heart and home—a fortune that cannot be lost. Try it, boys. Try it, men. Try it, women and girls. And if it don't turn out so, then I am much mistaken.

THE HYACINTH.

EMILY was grieved because the winter lasted so
long ; for she was fond of flowers, and had a
little garden, in which she raised some very beautiful ones, tending them with her own hands. Therefore she was very anxious that the winter might
pass away, and the pleasant spring return.

"Look, Emily !" said her father, "I have brought
thee a flower-root, a bulb, but thou must cultivate
it thyself with care."

"How can I, father ?" replied the maiden.
"Every thing is covered with snow, and the earth
is as hard as a stone."

Thus she spoke, for she did not know that flowers
might be reared in vases. But her father gave her
a vase filled with earth, and Emily placed the bulbs
therein. She looked, however, at her father and
smiled, doubtful whether he was in earnest in what
he had said ; for she imagined that flowers could
not thrive unless they had the blue sky above their
heads, and the mild breezes of spring about them.

In a few days the earth in the vase was raised,
and green leaves sprouted forth. Emily was over-
joyed, and she ran and told her father, her mother,
and the whole household, of the growth of the
young plant.

"How little is requisite," said her mother, "to

rejoice the heart, while it is still innocent and true to nature !"

Emily then sprinkled the plant with water, and smiled complacently upon it.

Her father observed her, and said : " That is right, my child. Rain and dew must be succeeded by sunshine. The beam of the benevolent eye giveth value to the bounty which the hand dispenses. Thy plant will be sure to thrive, Emily."

The leaves soon appeared entirely above the surface of the earth, and were ·of a beautiful green. Emily's joy was greater than ever. " Oh !" she exclaimed with an overflowing heart : "I shall be content, though it should not produce a single flower !"

" More will be given to thee," said her father, " than thou darest hope for. This is the reward of moderation, and of a heart that is content with little." He now showed her the germ of the flower, which lay hidden between the leaves.

Emily's care and attention increased every day, as the blossom gradually unfolded itself. With delicate hand she sprinkled it with water, and when a gleam of sunshine broke from the clouds, she carried the vase to the window, and her breath, light as the morning breeze that plays about the rose, blew away the dust that had settled upon the leaves.

" How sweet is the union of love and innocence !" said her mother.

Emily's thoughts were occupied with her flower, until she fell asleep at night, and as soon as she awoke in the morning. Often, too, in her dreams, she behold her hyacinth in full blossom, and when, in the morning, she found that it was not yet unfolded, she was not troubled, but said with a smile, " I must have patience a little longer."

Sometimes she would ask her father whether the flower would be of this or that color, and when she had enumerated all the colors, she would say cheerfully, " But it is all one to me, so it do but blossom !"

At length the blossom appeared. Early one morning twelve little bells were found expanded. They hung down in the full bloom of youthful beauty, between five broad leaves of emerald green. Their color was a pale red, like the rays of the glowing morn, or the delicate flush on Emily's cheek. The flower diffused around a fragrant odor. It was a bright morning in the month of March.

Emily's joy was calm and silent, as she bent over the flower, and gazed upon it. Her father approached, looked at his beloved child and at the hyacinth, and said : " Behold, Emily, what the hyacinth is to thee, that art thou to us !"

The maiden sprang up, threw herself into her father's arms, and, after a long embrace, she said, in a low voice : " Dear father ! oh, that I could rejoice your heart as you have rejoiced mine !"

ONLY WAITING.

ONLY waiting, till the shadows
   Are a little longer grown;
Only waiting, till the glimmer
   Of the day's last beam is flown;
Till the night of earth is faded,
   From the heart once full of day;

Till the stars of heaven are breaking
  Through the twilight soft and grey.

Only waiting, till the reapers
  Have the last sheaf gathered home ;
For the summer time is faded,
  And the autumn's winds have come,
Quickly, reapers, gather quickly
  The last ripe hours of my heart,
For the bloom of life is withered,
  And I hasten to depart.

Only waiting, till the angels
  Open wide the mystic gate,
At whose feet I long have lingered,
  Weary, poor, and desolate.
Even now, I hear the footsteps,
  And their voices far away ;
If they call me, I am waiting,
  Only waiting to obey,

Only waiting till the shadows
  Are a little longer grown ;
Only waiting, till the glimmer
  Of the day's last beam is is flown ;
Then from out the gathered darkness,
  Holy, deathless stars shall rise,
By whose light my soul shall gladly
  Tread its pathway to the skies.

YOUNG MEN.

THE idea is prevalent in some communities, that the young men are unfit for generals or states- men, and that they must be kept in the background until their physical strength is impaired by age, and their intellectual faculties blunted by years. Let us look at the history of the past, and from the long list of heroes and statesmen who have nobly dis- tinguished themselves, we will find that they were young men who performed those acts which have won for them an imperishable meed of fame, and which placed their names on the page of history. Alexander, the conqueror of the whole civilized world, viz. Greece, Egypt, and Asia, died at 33. Bonaparte was crowned Emperor of France when 33 years of age. Pitt, the younger brother, was 33 years of age, when in Britain's Parliament he boldly advocated the cause of the American Colo- nies; and but 22 when made Chancellor of the Exchequer. Edmund Burke, at the age of 25, was the First Lord of the Treasury. Our own Wash- ington was but 25 when he covered the retreat of the British at Braddock's defeat, and was appointed to be commander-in chief of all the Virginia forces. Alexander Hamilton, at 20, was a Lieutenant Col- onel and aid to Washington; at 25, a member of Congress, and at 32, Secretary of the Treasury. Thomas Jefferson was but 23 when he drafted the

ever-memorable Declaration of Independence. At
the age of 30 years, Sir Isaac Newton occupied the
mechanical chair at Cambridge College, England,
having by his scientific discoveries rendered his
name immortal.

ECHO ANSWERING.

"WHAT must be done to conduct a newspaper
right ?"—"write."

"Speaking of the Eastern war, one asked what
will be the expence ?"—"pence."

"What's necessary for a farmer to assist him ?"—
"system."

"What would give a blind man the greatest delight ?"—"light."

"What's the best counsel given by a justice of
the peace ?"—"peace."

"Who commits the greatest abominations ?"—
"nations."

"What cry is the great terrifier ?"—"fire."

"What are some women's chief exercise ?"—
"sighs."

"Who is more beautiful than she? I demand an
answer."—"Ann, sir."

CHICKENS.

LITTLE Jeannie's little chickens,
  Hear them pe-ep, pe-ep, peep!
Little fingers bring their dinner;
  Now they have a golden heap.

In her plump and dimpled fingers
  Jeannie takes the downy thing,
Laughs to see him fear, and flutter
  Such a funny "make-believe" wing.

"Pretty chick, I'll never hurt you;
  See, I bring you meal so nice;"
But the chick would hear no further—
  Off he scampered in a trice.

THE WAY TO DO IT.

As step by step, the hill we mount,
As, one by one, we learn to count,
So, word by word, we learn to spell,
And, line by line, to reading well.

TOBACCO.

WHAT think you a lad of sixteen said to us lately, when we remonstrated with him upon the
base indulgence of tobacco ?

"I don't smoke because I love it, *but because it's a
habit I can't overcome.*"

It was at the same time a very sad and a very
laughable excuse. Can't *overcome* it—a *boy*—can't
overcome the filthy habit of smoking cigars, and
chewing filthy tobacco ; would rather deny himself
the pleasure of decent company ; rather possess a
breath filled with the odor of corruption, than give
up the *pleasure* of sucking at one of the most nau-
seous compounds that man, in his foolishness ever
concocted.

We pity that boy—we pity anybody who has not
sufficient resolution to cast off a habit that he
acknowledges is hourly committing ravages upon
his health ; who suffers in numerous ways ; who
loses self-respect, allows his teeth to accumulate
offensive matter ; lounges in ungraceful postures ;
obliges every one to open the windows wherever he
goes, his own olfactory organs being deadened by
the constant effluvia, so that he is not aware how
great a nuisance he is ; gives up all refinement—for
who ever saw refinement in the midst of a puffing,
lolling, spitting circle ? Who ever saw refinement

in the low bar-room, the street-corner loungers, the mean, vile denizens of the most infamous haunts?

But what shall we do, when *infants* use the destructive agent—infants of six and seven years, some of whom smoke *manfully,* if that word pleases the grown-up sucklings?

Not long ago, a little boy, not seven years old, came into the house where we were staying, stupid and sick, reeling unsteadily, and fell, almost sense-less, upon the floor, causing great panic, as may be supposed. We found out the cause in a few moments. Another little boy, somewhat older, had coaxed him to smoke a few puffs on an old cigar, and the alarming *symptoms of poison* were the result of his first effort. Thus even babes are teaching one another, and it behooves parents to be on the watch, to guard these poor innocents from a habit that too often leads to infamy—that infamy cherish-es as one of her most darling sins.

READING.—Always have a book within your reach, which you may catch up at any odd minutes. Resolve to edge in a little reading every day, if it is but a single sentence. If you can give fifteen minutes a day, it will be felt at the end of the year. Thoughts take up no room. When they are right, they afford a portable pleasure, which one may travel or labor with, without any trouble or incum-brance.

JUST TOO LATE.

SEE that poor old man, with his valise and umbrella, hallooing after the stage coach with all his might, while it passes quietly on its way. He is just too late. If he had been one minute earlier he would have been in season, and would have been saved from a world of vexation and disappointment that now disturb his mind.

His name is Benjamin Bailey, an easy, inactive old man, who loves to tell stories and entertain his friends, and who never seems to have any clear conception that time is passing, or that it is any later now than it was six hours ago.

He is late to bed and late to rise, late to breakfast and late to work. On Sunday he is late to church, and if he has an appointment he is sure to be half an hour behind the time.

Rumor says says that when he was going to a distant state to be married he was two weeks in getting off, because he could not on any day get to the boat in season to start.

He has now packed his valise and is starting on a journey to transact very important business, and business requiring the utmost haste.

It seems that he has been engaged in a vexatious law suit, which has been carried up to its last appeal, and is about to be decided against him. He has just come in possession of important facts that might turn the case and save him from bankruptcy and ruin.

But there goes the stage and he is left behind, and cannot now, by any possible means, arrive in time to save the case.

Poor old man! all his raised hopes are dashed— He has lost his case, and lost his earthly all. How his heart throbs with unvailing regrets! How he wishes he had heeded the advice of his friends, who would have hurried his departure. But it is such an old habit with him to go close on time, that he would really be unhappy if he were by some chance to be five minutes too early. He has a sort of pride in delaying till the last moment and then barely escaping by a hair's breadth. But this foolish pride has cost him a great many disappointments and loss·

es, and has all his life long been his ruling star of evil.

The simple and beautiful habit of punctuality, formed when he was young and cherished through life, would have saved him and his family a world of trouble. But he is too old to be changed now, or to be effectually taught even by the bitter lessons of experience. His friends have long since abandoned the hope of any change. When one has arrived at his period of life he does not often throw off or essentially modify his old habits ; they have become a part of himself, and will cling to him till he rests in his grave.

How important, then, that the habits which we form in youth be such as we would wish to cherish in mature years—that they be such as will adorn and not mar our character.

Look again at that toiling and unhappy old man in the picture—his hat has blown off, and his head is bared to the breeze, while his heart is throbbing with disappointment and sorrow. While you feel a pity for his misfortune, learn, before your habits are unalterably fixed, to be punctual at all times. The habit, once formed, will have more to do than I can now tell or you can understand in shaping and perfecting your whole character. It will be worth more to you than an inherited fortune in stocks and acres, because it will be an element of real wealth within. Good habits, like the acquisitions of the mind, enrich the possessor with a real wealth, which is, and ever will be, his own, because a part of him-

POSITIVE AND COMPARATIVE.

THERE are lines written, simple and strange,
   Tragic, comic, pathetic, and narrative,
So I'll now turn my hand for a change
   To a positive and comparative.

The first English letter is A,
   We none of us live without air,
The prettiest month is called May,
   But the head of our city's a mayor.

A knock at the door is a rap,
   An over-all coat is a wrapper,
A belt made of leather's a strap,
   But a girl of six feet is a strapper !

The first rule in sums is to add,
   A venemous snake is an adder,
A boy of sixteen is a lad
   But a lamplighter's help is his ladder,

An apartment is also a room,
   A doubtful report is a rumor,
The blossoms of trees are their bloom,
   A short reign had poor Mrs. Bloomer !

The end of the day is called night,
   A drug of great virtue is nitre,
A very small insect's a mite,
   But a clergyman's hope is a mitre.

A cutter has only one mast,
   The ruler of Pembroke's " the Master,
The Great Exhibition is past,
   But a shepherd is also a pastor.

The fame of Old England is great,
  A scraper for spice is a grater,
A manner of walking is a gait
  But an over-all trowser's a gaiter.

To incline any way is to tend,
  A five-year's old fowl isn't tender,
I'll give you one more for the end,
  Saul called on the old witch of Endor.

———◆◆◆———

LIFE.

We are born—we laugh—we weep—
  We love—we droop—we die!
Ah! wherefore do we laugh, or weep?
  Why do we live, or die?
Who knows that secret deep?
  Alas! not I.

Why doth the violet spring
  Unseen by human eye?
Why doth the radiant seasons bring
  Sweet thoughts that quickly fly?
Why do our fond hearts cling
  To things that die?

We toil, through pain and wrong—
  We fight—and fly?
We love—we lose—and then, ere long.
  Cold and dead we lie!
O life! is *all* thy song
  "Endure and—die!"

HOPS AND BEANS;

THE WAY THEIR VINES RUN.

NOT more than two in a hundred, I am sure, have well learned the art of seeing. I doubt whether many people know that there is such an art. They overlook the most interesting facts, they don't see things right before them. We may refer to the vines of their gardens. They walk among them daily, without so much as suspecting that some of them are very particular as to the way they run.

"I am not sure that I understand you, sir. It sounds rather queer, that vines are particular which way they run. I always thought that they creep about in any direction, just where there is the most room, or the best chance to lay hold of a support."

You talk, John, pretty much as I expected. It is true that those vines which keep to the ground, seem satisfied to run to any one of a hundred points of the compass. It is true, also, that those which have an upward tendency, are apt to cling to whatever is most convenient. Still, they are very nice as to the manner in which they lay hold of their supports, and coil themselves around them. You needn't go far for the proof of this.

Here are some hop-vines. You will find, on examination, that they all take the same course—that in coiling around their respective poles, they all go from the east to the west by way of the south. Nor

can you force them to change their direction. If
you put them around the poles in reverse order, you
will find, before many days have passed, that they
have undone your work, and coiled themselves up
just as they were before you meddled with them.

Step across, now, to this patch of beans. These,
too, you observe, have a manifest choice in regard
to the route they take. Starting from the east,
again, every runner reaches the west by going
around by the north side of the pole. And they are
just as much determined to go in this direction as
are the hop-vines to go in the other. They will re-
sist all your attempts to train them to a different
course.

You see, then, that these plants are under law.
They are bound to a fixed method of growth and
development. They must take a definite direction,
as certainly as water must run down-hill. Nor is
this otherwise than we should expect. It is only
one of the innumerable instances of order and
method which appear in the works of God, and
which so powerfully illustrate his wisdom and goodness.

———

NO man who improves his leisure hours in reading and study, can fail of becoming distinguished and useful in his profession; while he who
spends his time in idleness or self-indulgence, is sure
to occupy an inferior position in life.

THE FLY.

WHAT a sharp little fellow is Mister Fly,
He goes where he pleases, low or high,
And can walk just as well with his feet to the sky
    As I can on the floor.
      At the window he comes,
  With a buzz and a roar,
      And o'er the smooth glass,
      Can easily pass,
  Or through the key-hole of the door.

He eats the sugar and goes away,
Nor even once asks what there is to pay,
And sometimes he crosses the tea-pot's steam
And comes and plunges his head in the cream;
Then on the edge of the jug he stands,
And cleans his wings with his feet and hands,
This done, through the window he hurries away,
And gives a buzz as if to say,
" At present I haven't a minute to stay,
But 'll peep in again in the course of the day,"

      Then away he'll fly,
        Where the sunbeams lie,
      And neither stop to shake hands,
      Nor bid one good bye :
Such a strange little fellow is Mister Fly,
Who goes where he pleases, low or high,
      And can walk on the ceiling
      Without even feeling
A fear of tumbling down " sky high."

LITTLE DOG TOBY AND THE WHITE PITCHER.

UST as likely as not, the MERRY children have a little dog at home. He may be black, or white, or brindled, or speckled, and he has a name to which he answers when called by it.

Well, I have a little dog, too, and he is yellow, and he has a large white spot on the side of his neck, and his name is Toby. He is about as large as a large cat, and he is very nimble in running and jumping.

We were taking tea, and Toby made himself a little too familiar by jumping up at one and then at another, so we had him put out into the kitchen.

Very soon we heard a loud threshing and knocking about the kitchen floor, and Toby began to scream and yell most piteously.

We thought he was in some mischief, and that Maggy, the little colored girl, was chastising him without due authority. Still there was no accounting for the knocking on the floor and around the room, accompanied by the screams of the poor little dog. The noise did not sound like that which would be made by a rat, or a cat, or another dog.

I ran to the kitchen door, and found it all dark. I called " Maggie, Maggie," and " Katy, Katy," but there was no Maggie nor Katy there, but Toby kept screaming, and the threshing on the floor was still going on.

I procured a light, and as I entered the room with the light in my hand, Toby made a desperate spring from under a chair, and leaped out upon the floor as though he had broken away from something that had hold of him.

Toby stopped screaming, and the knocking ceased. By the side of the chair laid a white earthen pitcher, in which there had been milk on the table.

The mystery was now solved. Toby had acquired a naughty way of jumping up in a chair, and so on to the table, and helping himself to whatever he could find that he liked. He ought to have been taught better, but so it was. These dogs, as well as boys and girls, will have some naughty tricks.

Toby, being shut out from the dining-room, as I have told you, thought he would make amends for the indignity, by climbing the table and helping himself in the dark.

What else he found I do not know, but it seems he had a desire for a little milk with his supper, and instead of turning the milk out into a cup, as is the proper way, he very clownishly thrust his head into the pitcher ; and when he had once got his head in there, he could not get it out. No doubt he was terribly frightened at his calamity, and so jumped down on the floor and ran around the room, threshing his pitcher and screaming most piteously, as we have already seen.

Toby was no doubt glad to get relieved by the help of the chair from his ugly nightcap, and I hope he will tell all the children to take care how they steal milk, or thrust their heads into pitchers that don't belong to them.

THE TWO WORLDS.

A land where sweetest roses fade,
 And smiling youth grows quickly old;
A land where sunshine turns to shade,
 And beauty takes a different mould;
A land of change, a land of care,
 Whose fleeting joys are little worth;
A land whose smile becomes a tear—
  That land is Earth!

A land of love where naught can sever,
 And beauty blooms with lustre fair;
A land where youth is young forever,
 For time exerts no influence there;
A land where streams of pleasure flow,
 And golden harps to all are given;
A land where we our God shall know—
  That land is Heaven!

LITTLE GRAVES.

THERE'S many an empty cradle,
   There's many a vacant bed,
There's many a lonely bosom,
   Whose joy and light is fled;
For thick in every graveyard
   The little hillocks lie—
And every hillock represents
   An angel in the sky.

A HINT FOR THE BOYS.

BOYS, truth is one of the richest jewels you can ever find, and one you should cherish as of priceless value. Many of your class have been lost to honor and greatness by disregarding its divine precepts, and have failed to become what they might have been, men of renown, by foolishly casting it away from their bosoms. All have this gem in the beginning, boys, but it may be lost by wickedness and carelessness ; if you have not lost it, and we hope you have not, let nothing cheat you out of it : for its equal is hardly to be found when lost.

Profane language, boys, is a sure index of a wicked heart and low breeding. Do you know a man or boy who commands respect from his neighbors? You never hear them swear—no oath ever trembles on their lips—emulate their bright example. Will you read the catalogue of sin and crime? You will find the disgraced actor to have been profane. Reflect on this, boys, and let no word of profanity escape your lips.

Beware of the company of such as haunt the tavern ; they may induce, over-persuade you to partake of the cup of shame and poison ; beware of them, " the tempting wine cup shun "—it will lead you to every sin, and disgrace you forever. Our word for it, boys, we are dealing in facts with you. Touch not a drop, for you may become a drunkard in the end, and you know how pitiful an object the poor drunkard is.

Be honest, be generous, be frank, be sober, be virtuous, abounding in truth, my boys, and you need not fear the consequences. Life is just opening her fitful path before you, but armed with these blessed traits you may rush fearlessly to the battle of life and fear no evil. You may be orphans, but if you have these as your jewels, you will meet with friends and encouragement in every lane of life. Men of business and wealth have their eyes upon you—watching you; they want clerks for their stores and apprentices for their workshops—if you have the virtues we have mentioned, they will not ask a better recommendation, but will choose you at once, taking you to their confidence and make men of you, and when they sleep in their graves, as all must, you may fill their places with honor and re-nown, as they have passed away. Boys, will you think of what we have been saying, and thinking, ACT?

————

An exchange says, says when David slew Goliah with a sling, the latter fell *stone dead,* and of course, quite astonished, as such a thing never entered his head before!

NEVER GIVE UP.

NEVER give up! it is wiser and better
   Always to hope, than once to despair ;
Fling off the load of Doubt's cankering fetter,
   And break the dark spell of tyrannical care :
Never give up! or the burden may sink you—
   Providence kindly has mingled the cup,
And in all trials and troubles, bethink you,
   The watchword of life must be, Never give up !

Never give up ! there are chances and changes
   Helping the hopeful, a hundred to one ;
And through the chaos High Wisdom arranges
   Ever success, if you'll only hope on ;
Never give up ! **for** the wisest is boldest,
   Knowing that providence mingles the cup,
And of all maxims, the best, as the oldest,
   Is the true watchword of Never give up !

Never give up ! though the grape shot may rattle
   Or the full thunder cloud over you burst,
Stand like **a** rock—and the **storm or the** battle
   Little shall harm you, though doing their worst :
Never give up ! if adversity presses,
   Providence wisely has mingled the cup,
And the best counsel, in all your distresses,
   Is the stout watchword of Never give up !

READ THIS BOYS.

TWO WAYS OF TELLING A STORY.

IN one of the most populous cities of New England, a year since, a party of lads, all members of the same school, got up a grand sleigh-ride. The sleigh was a large and splendid one, drawn by six grey horses.

On the day following the ride, as the teacher entered the school-room, he found his pupils in high merriment, as they chatted about the fun and frolic of their excursion. In answer to some inquiries which he made about the matter, one of the lads volunteered to give an account of their trip and its incidents.

As he drew near the end of his story, he exclaimed, " O, sir ! there was one little circumstance that I had almost forgotten. As we were coming home, we saw a queer looking affair in the road. It proved to be a rusty old sleigh, fastened behind a covered wagon, proceeding at a very slow rate, and taking up nearly the whole road.

" Finding the owner was not disposed to turn out, we determined upon a volley of snowballs and a good hurrah. They produced a right effect, for the crazy machine turned out in the deep snow, and the skinny old pony started in a full trot.

" As we passed, some one gave the old jilt of a horse a good crack, which made him run faster than

he ever did before, I'll warrant.   And so, with
another volley of snowballs pitched into the front
part of the wagon, and with three-times-three cheers,
we rushed by.

"With that, an *old fellow* in the wagon, who was
buried up under an old hat, and who dropped the
reins, bawled out. 'Why don't you turn out, then ?'
says the driver. So we gave him three rousing
cheers more. His horse was frightened again, and
ran up against a loaded team, and I believe almost
capsized the old creature : and so we left him."

"Well, boys," replied the instructor, "take your
seats, and I will take my turn and tell you a story,
all about a sleigh-ride, too. Yesterday afternoon a
very venerable old clergyman was on his way from
Boston to Salem, to pass the residue of the winter
at the house of his son. That he might be prepared
for journeying in the spring, he took with him his
wagon, and for the winter the sleigh, which he
fastened behind the wagon.

"His sight and hearing were somewhat blunt by
age, and he was proceeding very slowly and quietly,
for his horse was old and feeble like his owner. His
thoughts reverted to the scenes of his youth, of his
manhood, and of his riper years. Almost forgetting
himself in the multitude of his thoughts, he was suddenly disturbed and terrified by loud hurrahs from
behind, and by a furious pelting upon the top of his
wagon.

"In his trepidation he dropped his reins, and as

his aged and feeble hands were quite benumbed
with cold, he could not gather them up, and his
horse began to run away. In the midst of the old
man's troubles, there rushed by him, with loud
shouts, a large party of boys, in a sleigh drawn by
six horses. 'Turn out ! turn out, old fellow !' 'Give
us the road, old boy !' 'What will you take for
your pony, old daddy ?' 'Go it, frozen nose ?'
'What's the price of oats ?' were the various cries
that met his ear.

" ' Pray do not frighten my horse !' exclaimed the
infirm driver. ' Turn out, then ! turn out !' was the
answer ; which was followed by repeated cracks and
blows from the long whip of the ' grand sleigh,'
with showers of snowballs, and three tremendous
cheers from the bo s that were in it. The terror of
the old man and his horse was increased, and the
latter ran away with him, to the imminent danger of
his life. He contrived, however, to secure his
reins, and to stop his horse just in season to prevent
his being dashed against a loaded team.

" A short distance brought him to his journey's
end, the house of his son. His old horse was comfortably housed and fed, and he himself abundantly
provided for. That son, boys, is your instructor,
and that *old fellow* and *old boy* (who did not turn out
for you, but who would gladly have given you the
whole road had he heard your approach), that *old
daddy* and *frozen nose*, was your master's father !"

Some of the boys buried their heads behind their

desks ; some cried, and many hastened to the teacher with apologies and regrets without end. All were freely pardoned ; but were cautioned that they should be more civil for the future to inoffensive travelers, and more respectful to the aged and infirm.

---◆◆◆---

THE OTHER HOME.

LIFE is full of doubt and sorrow ;
　All that's beautiful must die :
Joyous smiles to-day—to-morrow
　Bitter tears—a heartfelt sigh.
All we ever love and cherish.
　But reminds it cannot stay,
And our brightest hopes will perish
　In the morning of their day.

Never more! it wakes an echo,
　Half of joy and half of pain ;
Visions rise in quick succession,
　Never will be mine again!
There was one best loved and truest,
　Ever near in days of yore—
Went to rest down in the churchyard
　I shall meet her never more !

In the land beyond the river,
　Farewell echoes never come :
Life is but a journey thither,
　To that other, brighter home !
Though our feet too often falter,
　Treading in the weary way,
Let a pure faith guide us ever,
　Till we reach the realms of day

KITE-FLYING.

" SAY, George, did you ever see a kite
Soar up to the clouds, and out of sight?"
" Indeed," said George. " you must think me green,
When out of sight, how could it be seen."

" Ah I there you have me," said Charles—" a hit—
I cannot cope with your ready wit,
So we'll drop it there, and see how high
We can get our beautiful kite to fly.

" Come, boys, hurra I away to the hill,
The breeze is free, our kite to fill,
The string is long, and shan't we be proud
To see her piercing yon floating cloud."

Then off they went at a joyous pace,
The kite shot up with bird-like grace,
As the string ran out, the ambitious kite,
Had entered the cloud, and was out of sight.

Huzza! Huzza! shouted one and all—
But pride must always come to a fall—
The mist-soaked paper fell off, and the frame
Followed its tail, and earthward came.

Well, now, I see, said Charles, with a sigh,
There is such a thing as flying *too high*,
And indeed it is nothing to make one proud,
When there's light around to be had in a cloud.

THE BIBLE.

Upon a mount a tree doth stand,
　　Heavy with fruit of gold,
And it is seen through all the land
　　Shining far in pictures bold.
Many there came from every land,
　　To seek for the precious ore,
They shook the tree with earnest hand,
　　And its fruits away they bore;

Yet its riches are never gone,
　　And the tree is never bare;
When e'er the precious fruit falls down,
　　Other fruits instead appear.
What is it called? and, if on earth,
　　Where, I ask, where can it be?
And who has seen and known its worth?
　　The precious Bible is the tree!

PERSEVERANCE—ITS VALUE.

ABOUT ten years ago, there was a little newsboy—very little for his age, which was fourteen

years—who sold papers at the corner now occupied
by the "Tribune" building and its adjuncts. This
boy, owing to his cheerful countenance, his proverb-
ial integrity, his industry—in brief, his good quali-
ties generally, made friends for himself everywhere,
and particularly among publishers. He did a very
good business. but his position did not suit him. We
advised him to go into a store.

"I can neither read nor write," responded he,
mournfully.

"Apprentice yourself to some trade, then," was
our advice.

"I think I will," he exclaimed, with a brightening
eye, and flushed check; "I think I will;" and off
he bounded.

We lost sight of him after this, and finally forgot
that such a being existed.

About a week ago, an athletic, well dressed young
man, with a ferocious pair of whiskers, and a brace
of merry, twinkling optics, that betokened a good
heart, and the best of health, stopped us in the
street, and, extending his hand, called us by name.

"Really, sir, you have the advantage of me."

"Not know ——— the little newsboy!" he cries,
as if astonished.

Truly it was our little newsboy. He had taken
our early advice, and had apprenticed himself to a
machinist.

"Where are you working?"

"Oh, I don't work now," was his proud answer;

"I own a saw mill on Long Island, and am doing business for myself. I have been my own boss a year. I bought out my concern with the savings of eight years ; I have a wife and two children, and my own cottage, and garden for them to live and delve in, and am as happy as the day is long. I can read and write, too," he continued, smiling with an air of triumph.

mm

KINDNESS.—Would it not please you to pick up a string of pearls, drops of gold, diamonds, and precious stones, as you pass along the street? It would make you feel happy for a month to come. Such happiness you can give to others. How, do you ask ? By dropping sweet words, kind remarks, and pleasant smiles as you pass along. These are true pearls and precious stones which can never be lost ; of which none can deprive you. Speak to that orphan child ; see the diamonds drop from her cheeks. Take the hand of that friendless boy ; bright pearls flash in his eyes. Smile on the sad and the dejected ; a joy diffuses his cheek more brilliant than the most splendid precious stones. By the way side, mid the city's din, and at the fireside of the poor, drop words to cheer and bless. You will feel happier when resting on your pillow at the close of the day, than if you had picked up a score of perishing diamonds. The latter fade and crumble in time ; the former grow brighter with age, and produce happier reflections forever.

JOHN RANDOLPH OUTDONE.

OF the many amusing anecdotes of this eccentric man of Roanoke, we do not believe the following was ever in print :

He was traveling through a part of Virginia in which he was unacquainted—and stopped during the night at the inn near the forks of the road. The inn-keeper was a fine old gentleman, and no doubt one of the first families of the Old Dominion. Knowing who his distinguished guest was, he endeavored during the evening to draw him into conversation, but failed in all his efforts. But in the morning, when Mr. Randolph was ready to start, he called for his bill, which on being presented was paid. The landlord, still anxious to have some conversation with him, began as follows :

" Which way are you traveling, Mr. Randolph ?"

" Sir," said Mr. Randolph, with a look of dis-pleasure.

" I asked," said the landlord, " which way are you traveling ?"

" Have I paid you my bill ?"

" Yes."

" Do I owe you anything more ?"

" No."

" Well, I am going just where I please—do you understand ?"

The landlord by this time got somewhat excited and Mr. Randolph drove off. But to the landlord's surprise in a few minutes the servant returned to inquire for his master which of the forks of the road to take. Mr. Randolph, not being out of hearing distance, the landlord spoke out, at the top of his breath, "Mr. Randolph, you don't owe me one cent; just take which road you please."

WHISTLING.

BOYS, we believe in whistling—we love to hear it. The boy or man at the plough, at the bench, or any other place where whistling may be tolerated, indicates that he is contented, that he is happy, and that he has music in his soul and on his lips, when your hear him whistling. Those who despise whistling should try to catch all the bobolinks and mocking birds, to prevent them from making music. Whistling is a happy institution; the boy or man who whistles works more willingly and constantly than the one who whistles not—he shows that he has a cheerful heart under his shirt front.

Mean, selfish, jealous men, never whistle. Did you ever hear an angry person whistling? Look to it boys—we will wait for the answer.

THE FIRST SNOW OF THE SEASON.

HEIGHO! brother Henry, what's **there,**
    Coming down by the bend of **the** road?

'Tis the old mammoth sleigh, I declare—
    Six horses! and oh! what a load!

I wish we were going, don't you?
    Oh me! what glorious fun!

Not so funny, dear Georgie—wet through
    By the fast falling snow, every one!

Oh! never mind that. I'd away,
    If I could, without being drowned.

But the **snow** is not deep, and the sleigh
    Cuts through, every step, to the ground.

Well, I wish they would just take me in;
    I would go, though you'd think me a fool.

No, brother, I would say 'twas a sin,
    For 'twould be playing truant from school.

I didn't mean that. But, you know,
    I never would go without leave.

Well, let us then hasten to go,
    It is time we were there, I perceive.

There's the stage going out upon wheels,
Don't you think they'll stick fast in the plain?

Perhaps not, brother George, **for it feels**
  As if snow **was** now turning to rain.

Well, it is rather damp—but then
    It is first-rate snow **for a ball.**

At the recess, at half past ten,
    We'll have a set-to, one and all.

THE FAMILY UNBROKEN.

NO thought is sweeter than that in heaven the
family shall be unbroken. All shall be there,
father, mother, brother, sister. No one absent. No
tie of love broken. No heart-ache, no mourning, no
sad longing for some dear one far away. The love
circle is complete. Each member in its place, filling
the hearts of all others, will give and receive the
charm of fullness. So it will be in all families. It
is a religion of love, a faith of the heart, as well the
head. It is that for which the whole soul longs.

" You have two children," said I.

" I have four," was the reply. " Two on earth,
two in heaven."

There spoke the mother! Still hers! only "gone
before!" Still remembered, loved, and cherished
by the hearth and at the board; their places not
yet filled; even though their successors draw life
from the same faithful breast where *their* dying
heads were pillowed.

" Two in heaven!"

Safely housed from storm and tempest; no sickness there; nor drooping head, nor fading eye, nor
weary feet, By the green pastures, tended by the
Good Shepherd, linger the little lambs of the heavenly fold.

" Two in heaven!"

Earth is less attractive! Eternity nearer! Invisible cords drawing the maternal soul upward. "Still, small" voices, ever whispering *Come!* to the world-weary spirit.

"Two in heaven!"

Mother of angels! Walk softly! holy eyes watch thy footsteps! cherub forms bend to listen! Keep thy spirit free from earth's taint; so shalt thou "go to them," though "they may not return to thee."

THE DRUNKARD'S WILL.

I LEAVE to society a ruined character, wretched example, and memory that will soon rot.

I leave to my parents, during the rest of their lives, as much sorrow as humanity, in a feeble and decrepid state, can sustain.

I leave to my brothers and sisters as much mortification and injury as I could well bring on them.

I leave to my wife a broken heart, a life of wretchedness, a shame to weep over me, premature death.

I give and bequeath to each of my children, poverty, ignorance, a low character, and the remembrance that their father was a monster.

HELPING MOTHER.

"THAT'S right, my son, so you would rather hold the thread for your mother to wind, than go and play with the boys in the street," said Mr. Stanley. "Yes, sir," replied Johnny, "I would rather help her as long as she needs me, then I can go and play and enjoy it."

"That's the boy for me," said Mr. Stanley to me in a low tone, "I shall keep an eye on that boy; when he grows up, I would rather have him in my store than nine-tenths of the boys, for the boy that loves to do as his mother wishes him, will be faithful to his employees."

Mr. Stanley passed on to his office, for he was a wealthy merchant, and had many clerks under him,

and I watched Johnny till the thread was all wound,
and several other things were done for "mother,"
then he asked, "is there anything else, mother?" and
she answered "no, my son, you can go and play
awhile now," and away he bounded with a light and
joyous heart, singing that beautiful song,

> "I ought to love my mother,
>   She loved me long ago :
> There is on earth no other
>   That ever loved me so.
> When a weak babe, much trial
>   I caused her, and much care,
> For me no self-denial
>   Nor labor did she spare."

I watched those boys at play, and could not but
notice the difference with which they entered into
the sport. Johnny entered into the exciting game
with all the love of a warm enthusiastic nature—he
had a quiet conscience within—he had done his duty,
and he could enjoy it ; but his companions who stole
away from home without helping their mothers, or
wilfully left against their express commands, had
but little true pleasure. If any thing went wrong,
they were sure to speak cross and were inclined to
grumble at almost everything. They were idlers
too, because they would not work, and could not
play with any enjoyment. What says the poet ?

> Don't stand in your tracks doing nothing but grumble,
> But start with a run if you meet with a tumble ;
> You had better be scoured by rubs in the dust
> Than to be in your idleness eaten by rust.

You will find this true, boys, that he who does cheerfully what his parents require, enjoys his play very much more than he who disobeys and tries to have his own way. And then, when you grow up, and want to find friends, remember that he who loves to "help mother," will always find warm friends to help him along in the world. Try it boys and girls, and you will find it so.

FRANKLIN'S MODE OF LENDING MONEY.

"I SEND you herewith a bill of ten louis-d'ors. I do not pretend to give much—I only lend it to you. When you return to your country, you can not fail of getting into some business that will, in time, enable you to pay all your debts. In this case, when you meet another honest man, in similar distress, you will pay me by lending this money to him, enjoining him to discharge the debt by a like operation, when he shall be able, and meet with such another opportunity. I hope it may pass through many hands, before it meet, with a knave to stop its progress. This is a trick of mine to do a great deal of good with a little money. I am not rich enough to spend much in good works, and am obliged to be cunning, and make the most of a little."

COLD WATER SONG.

THE bright sparkling waters
  That gush from the hills,
And gladden the valley's
  With streamlets and rills,
Oh! they never, never fail,
  But with laughter and song,
From springtide till springtide,
  They're flashing along.

There's life in their sweetness,
  There's health in their flow,
And they whisper of heaven
  Wherever they go;
And they scatter, scatter wide
  The treasures they bear,
As pure as the sunshine,
  As free as the air.

Come, then, all who hear me,
  To fountains divine,
Touch, taste not, nor handle
  Gin, brandy, or wine.
They wither, wither all,
  Bud, blossom, and fruit,
But the bright sparkling waters
  Are health to the root.

They gush without money,
  They flow without price,
To the hut of the beggar,   '
  The hovel of vice—
They're laden, laden richly
  With promise of wealth,
And insure to the temperate
  Contentment and health.

LEARNING TO DRAW.

DRAWING.

DRAWING is an imitative art by which the forms, positions, and relations of objects are represented on a flat surface.

The faculties employed in this and in other imitative arts are possessed in a certain degree by all persons. Some possess these faculties in so high a degree as to indicate a decided genius for such pursuits, and if they give practice to their skill they will become celebrated.

The majority, however, are not so endowed as to be able without instruction and considerable practice to draw with very great skill.

The practice of elementary drawing at school, has been, until recently, too much neglected, and in but few instances now does it receive the share of attention that it deserves. Drawing has not been considered an essential part of a good education, consequently but few have received instruction.

But tastes are changing, and the time is near, when the ability to sketch with a moderate degree of accuracy will be indispensable to a finished education. It is a beautiful accomplishment, and will well reward all the labor we expend in learning to draw.

In many situations, when wandering in our own or in foreign lands, we see objects, of which we would be glad to carry away some memorandum, and of which a slight pencil sketch would be sufficient to perpetuate the vision and even to communicate it to others.

It is a sad pity that for want of a few elementary lessons and slight practice, we should lose the pleasure of perpetuating in pictures the beautiful objects which we meet. In this view drawing is like writing—the one communicates by pictures, the other by written words. The former is often the most impressive, and conveys a sentiment and a meaning which written words could never tell.

Drawing is effected by various materials, as chalk black lead, or India ink. Simple drawings are made on white paper, or Bristol board. One should commence the study of the art by acquiring a free and easy use of the hand. For this purpose, drawing lines with chalk on a black board is a very good exercise. After you have acquired an easy use of the hand, and can readily draw straight and curved lines, you may begin by copying other drawings. This is only allowable in beginners, and is intended to make them familiar with the manner in which lines answer the purpose of representation.

To be master of the art you must throw aside all copy-books, and learn to draw by your own ingenuity from tangible objects in nature and art. In this study the hand is taught to obey the conceptions of the mind. When, for example, we see a house, or a tree, we observe its shape or figure, its lines and angles, or curves. We then take a pencil, and bending the mind intensely on the form of the object, we define it in visible lines on paper. The more perfectly the hand can obey the impulse of the mind when bent on a definite object, the more true and correct will the drawing appear.

But, for directions in drawing, reference must be had to books on the subject, and to competent teachers.

If by a word of suggestion we shall be able to stimulate a taste for this beautiful art in any one of our readers, the object of the article will be attained.

LITTLE BY LITTLE.

"LITTLE by little," said a thoughtful boy,
"Moment by moment I'll well employ,
Learning a little every day,
And not spending all my time in play;
And still this rule in my mind shall dwell,
' Whatever I do, I will do it well.'

"Little by little, I'll learn to know
The treasured wisdom of long ago;
And one of these days perhaps we'll see
That the world will be the better for me."
And do you not think that this simple plan
Made him a wise and a useful man?

WHAT SAITH THE FOUNTAIN.

WHAT saith the fountain,
　　Hid in the glade,
Where the tall mountain
　　Throweth its shade?

" Deep in my waters, reflected serene,
All the soft beauty of heaven is seen ;
Thus let thy bosom, from wild passions free,
Ever the mirror of purity be."

What saith the streamlet,
　　Flowing so bright,
Clear as a beamlet,
　　Of silvery light?

" Morning and evening still floating along,
Upward forever ascendeth my song ;

Bo thou contented, whate'er may befall,
Cheerful in knowing that God is o'er all,"

What saith the river,
 Majestic in flow,
Moving forever
 Calmly and slow ?

" Over my surface the great vessels glide,
Ocean-ward borne by my strong heaving tide ;
Toil on, my brother, life vanisheth fast,
Labor unwearied, rest cometh at last."

What saith the ocean,
 Boundless as night,
Ceaseless in motion,
 Resistless in might ?

" Fountain to streamlet, streamlet to river,
All in my bosom commingle forever ;
Morning to noontide, noontide to night,
Soon will eternity veil thee from sight,"

ADVICE TO YOUTH.

IN climbing a ladder, always look up — never down, for in doing the latter a fall is imminent. So in life : aim to keep company with those above you, rather than those beneath you, in intellectual capacity and acquirement. Emulate your superiors. If you can't find them, you are blind ; if you won't find them, you are not fit for their society, and better at once turn your ears, and immerse your muddy faculties in the mysteries of poudrette or putty making.

THE WAY TO BE HAPPY.

A HERMIT there was,
  And he lived in a grot,
And the way to be happy,
  They said he had got.
And I wanted to learn it,
  I went to his cell,
And when I came there,
  The old hermit said, " Well,
Young man, by your looks,
  You want something, I see,
Now tell me the business
  That brings you here ?

" The way to be happy,
  They say you have got.
And as I want to learn it,
  I've come to your grot,
Now I beg and entreat,
  If you *have* such a plan,
That you'll write it me down,
  As plain as you can."
Upon which the old hermit
  Went to his pen,
And brought me this note
  When he came back again.

" 'Tis *being*, and *doing*
  And *having*, that make
All the pleasures and pains,
  Of which things partake,
To *be* what God pleases—
  To *do* a man's best,
And to *have* a good heart—
  Is *the way* to be *blest.*

THE CHINESE OPIUM SMOKER.

A CHINESE opium smoker! Have you, young
reader, ever seen one? Do you know what his
character is? Perhaps not. Here then is the picture of one for you to look at. If you will examine
the picture closely, you will see that the person represented is not a common citizen, but an officer of
the gevernment. You may know this from his cap,
which hangs upon a kind of ornamented tripod,
standing upon the table; from the long string of
beads, which hangs from his shoulders down in
front; and from the square piece of figured silk, at-

tached to his dress in front, which is partly covered by his hand in holding his pipe. The opium smoker usually lies down, while smoking, that he may conveniently sleep off the drowsy effects of the drug ; for the smoking commonly puts its victim to sleep, and he will often fall asleep and wake up several times at a single smoking.

But we must now tell you how this officer became an opium smoker. He was probably, in the first instance, invited, as an act of politeness, to smoke with some friend ; it being fashionable in China to offer a friend the opium pipe, just as it is thought to be in some circles in this Christain land to offer a guest a glass of wine, or of some other spirituous liquor. This officer probably accepted the invitation of his friend, and found the effects of the pipe very exhilarating and pleasant. This induced him to try it again, and to continue the practice for a few days ; when, alas ! he found he had contracted a habit, which he could not throw off, without serious consequences to his health, and perhaps, not without endangering his life. Yes, my young friends, such is the inevitable lot of those who indulge in the luxury of the opium pipe for only a few times, or a few days. A habit is formed, far more inveterate than the habit of drinking ardent spirits. The victim of the habit feels compelled to indulge it, as a means of preserving his health, if not his life. He knows of no medicine, which would prevent his suffering severe pain and disease, if he should cease

smoking or fail to be *regular to the hour*. If, for
example, he has smoked every day at nine o'clock
in the morning for a fortnight, his habit has become
so fixed, that he *must* smoke at that hour, whatever
may be his circumstances or occupation. He cannot defer the indulgence till ten o'clock, for a single
day, without exposure to very severe pain. Does
he not, then, make a fatal mistake, when he indulges
in the use of the pipe for the first time? Can the
friend, who offers him the pipe as an act of politeness, be innocent in respect to his pitiable condition?

Do you now wish to know what is the character
of the opium smoker? Or what is the result of the
habit which he has formed? This is painful to de-
scribe. It is not easy to conceive of any thing more
so; for the effects of the opium smoking are disas-
trous in the extreme. It leads men to be careless
in respect to their personal habits; negligent and
even incapable of attending to their business; in-
different to the interests of their families and
friends; and reckless in respect to moral character.
The victim, as we have already intimated, is the
slave of his habit; and in serving it, he loses his
health; he loses his property; he loses his self-respect and his character. As he passes before you, his
appearance is haggard and wretched; his features
pale and his system emaciated; his step is not firm,
and, did you not know to the contrary, you might
think he was suffering from extreme poverty, and
the advanced stages of consumption. Should you

CHINESE MANDARINS.

follow him to his home, while you might not find
him cross and savage, you would see him careless
and thoughtless of the welfare of his family. We
have been told, on good authority, that he sometimes sells, not only the clothing of his wife and
children, but also wife and children themselves, in
order to obtain means to supply himself with opium.
Opium he must have, and there is scarcely a crime,
which he will not commit in cases of necessity, to
procure it. And in many cases, the end of the
whole business is beggary and premature death.

Of the number of those addicted to opium smoking, in China, we have no data for forming a correct estimate. Frequent inquiries of the Chinese
themselves, have afforded no definite information in
this respect. Some have said, one-half of the adult
population; others have said two-fifths; some three-
fifths; and some have made the proportion as high
as four-fifths. What the true proportion is, we know
not. But we do know that the number of those
who have fallen under the dominion of this destructive habit is very large. No doubt the aggregate
would embrace several millions. And these are
most of them from the fathers and husbands of the
families of the Celestial Empire; they are those
who ought to be the support and comfort of those
whom Providence has placed under their care; but
who have been made by opium a plague and a curse
in the home circle.

There is one more inquiry, which arises here, and

demands attention.   Who furnishes the Chinese
with opium ?   And where does it come from ?   We
must answer these questions briefly.   The opium is
raised in India, under the direction of the East India Company, to which it is a source of very great
profit.   By this Company it is sold to English and
American merchants, the representatives of the two
pricipal Christain nations of the world, and also to
the merchants of some other countries.   These merchants take it to the coast of China, and sell it at a
great profit to themselves, and that in despite of the
laws of the Chinese Empire, prohibiting the impor-
tation of the drug, and without regard to the untold
amount of wretchedness and woe which it brings
upon that vast nation.   And now, who is responsible
for that wretchedness and woe ?   Whose is the
guilt ?   Will not he who sells the opium, as well as
he who uses it, have a fearful account to render at
the bar of the civilized world, and at the higher
Court of Eternal Justice ?   And if those, who desire to promote good morals in this Christain land,
feel it incumbent upon them to adopt stringent
measures to prevent men from selling ardent spirits,
ought they not also to do something to prevent merchants, from this same Christain nation, selling
opium to the Chinese, among whom it is producing
such incalculable evil and misery ?   Let sober con-
victions answer this question.

TEACHING UNDER DIFFICULTIES.

"WHAT is that?" asked Mrs. Farley,
    Pointing to great O.
"That's my hoop," said willful Charley,
    " Can't you make it go?"
"No, my darling, don't talk so,
    That's the letter O.

"Now, what's that, my little duck?
    Charlie, dear, be good."
"That, mamma, is father's buck,
    When he's sawing wood."
" Charlie, dear, don't mother vex,
    You must call that X.

"Now, my darling, here's a kiss"
    (Love is wisdom's germ)—
" Charlie, tell me what is this."

"Mamma, that's a worm."
"No," said Mrs. F., with stress,
"Well, you know 'tis S.

"Now, my pet, I'll try you here—
Charlie, be a man—
Tell me what is that, my dear,"
"That is sissy's fan."
"Charles, how naughty you can be!
Sure you know that's V."

———•••———

Love met a fair child,
Tripping lightly along;
With a look meek and gentle
She warbled this song—

"O Birdie, O Birdie,
That sits on a tree,
I often do wonder
What's Sunday to thee.

"Your voice is so sweet
All that holy day long,
That it oft makes me think
There is praise in your song."

Love threw down his quiver—
He caught the sweet maid;
And now both together
They sit in the shade.

WORK, BUT DON'T WORRY.

WORK, work, but don't worry, oh no, oh no ;
The less you hurry the faster you'll go :
All worry, no work standeth still in the fire ;
All work, and no worry soon wins his desire.

Work, work, it is hearty ; but worry looks pale ;
In his eye there's a wildness, its vigor doth fail,
It's nerve is not firm, nor its footsteps so free ;
Work, work, and not worry, is that which suits me.

Work, work, hearty work ! see what it hath wrought,
For right and for truth what battles hath fought ;
What blessings hath won, and what benefits given,
For man, and the workers on earth and in heaven.

But worry, poor worry ! say what hath it done,
But to flutter abroad, and repine when alone ?
It hath stung its own heart, and dug its own grave,
But ever been powerless to bless or to save.

Work, work, saith Scripture ; but worry, nowhere ;
Faith, faith it enjoins, and forbids every care ;
With labors of love the hands it would fill,
And the peace of the Lord on the spirit distil.

Work, work, how it thickens ! Yet do what you can
In patience and gladness, with the heart of a man
The workers shall joy when the work is all o'er ;
Work on, fellow-worker, but worry no more.

THE WREATH.

ONE bright evening, as I was wandering in the beautiful woods of W———, I suddenly came upon a group of children.

Two little girls were busily employed in twining a wreath of the many richly tinted flowers which they had gathered as they had passed along.

Another little girl, the youngest, whose bright hair fell around her in a shower of golden curls, and for whom the wreath was evidently intended, was flitting about from one to the other, in a state of restless delight ; now assisting her little brother to arrange the flowers, and now handing them to her sisters for the wreath. I did not like to interrupt them ; and yet, wishing to see the little girl crowned with her beautiful wreath, I sat down be-

neath a tree, where I could observe all that passed
without being perceived by the little party.

I had not been there long, when one of the little
girls called out in a very distressed tone of voice,
"Oh, Ernest! Ernest! do come here, and kill this
horrid earwig! do be quick." Ernest, a tall, man-
ly-looking boy, whom I had not before observed,
came forward with a book in his hand, which he
laid down, and said kindly, as he took away the
offending insect—

Why, Annie, dear, you are too old to be afraid of
an earwig ; and, besides, you should not call it horrid, for you know God made it as well as you, and
nothing which he has made can be horrid. Neither
should you wish me to kill it, simply because you do
not like it, for you know we should never take away
the life of anything, unless it is absolutely necessary,
and we cannot avoid doing so. And do you know,
Annie, this horrid earwig, as you call it, is, in real-
ity, very beautiful ; for though we cannot now see
them, he has a pair of exquisite thin gauze wings,
shaped like an ear, from which he derives his name
of earwing, which has been corrupted into earwig."

" Oh," said the other little girl, I wish I could
see his wings, "I did not know that earwigs had
any ; do, Ernest, make him show them ?"

" I cannot, now, dear," he replied ; " but when
we go home we will ask papa to lend us his micro-
scope, and then you will see them very plainly.

But come, are you not ready to go now, for it is getting late?"

"Oh yes," said Annie, "we have just finished Edith's wreath. Here, Edith, darling; come and let me put it on for you. There! is it not beautiful, Ernest?"

Ernest gave a very approving look, and little Edith said—

"Oh yes, it *is* beautiful; thank you, dear Annie! and Carrie, too, for having made it for me;" and the put up her little mouth for a kiss, whilst her loving blue eyes sparkled with delight, as, taking her little brother's hand, she said—

"Come, Willie! let us run on and show mamma how gay I am; they walk so slow, I can't keep pace with them."

"How nice it is, Ernest," said Annie, "to make other persons happy. I am sure it has given us far more pleasure to make that wreath for Edith, than if we had made it for ourselves; has it not Carrie?"

"Yes," I thought, as their happy voices died away in the distance, "how nice it is to make other persons happy." How I wished that all people would, like little Annie, think so too; for if they would, how much pain and sorrow, from unkind words and actions, would be avoided! Do not you think so, too, little reader? and will not you try to be kind and gentle, and endeavor to make all around you happy?

THE SOUHEGAN RIVER.

TEN leagues in length, among the hills,
  A little river winds its way,
Fed by a hundred brooks and rills,
  It keeps on flowing night and day

Along its banks fresh pastures grow,
  And laughing fields of corn and grain ;
And thirsty sheep and cattle know
  Where WATER is ne'er sought in vain.

Shrewd anglers, crouching by its side,
  Catch pickerel, eel, and speckled trout;
And on its winter-frozen tide,
  The schoolboy's skates swift mark their rout.

A dozen mills its current turns,
  Where spindles whirl, and looms keep time ;
Or rumbling stones grind up the corn,
  Or saws and lathes perpetual chime.

Six thriving villages have grown
  Near by this little river's side,
And happy thousands gladly own
  How much they owe their patron's tide.

Reader, whoever thou may'st be,
These lines are written unto thee ;
Their lesson scan, their moral heed,
And follow where their teachings lead.

If rivers ne'er forget to flow
And scatter blessings where they go,
Why should'st thou spend an idle life,
Or vex the earth with selfish strife ?

Rather, each day, by word and deed,
Do GOOD to those who stand in need;
And thousands yet shall bless thy name,
And hand it down to honest fame.

* * *

TRY, TRY AGAIN.

'Tis a lesson you should heed—
        Try, try again.
If at first you don't succeed,
        Try, try again,
Then your courage should appear;
For, if you will persevere,
You will conquer, never fear,
        Try, try again.

Once or twice, though you should fail,
        Try, try again.
If you would at last prevail,
        Try, try again.
If we strive, 'tis no disgrace,
Though we may not win the race.
What should we do in such a case?
        Try, try again.

If you find your task too hard,
        Try, try again.
Time will bring you your reward;
        Try, try again.
All that other folks can do,
Why with patience should not you?
Only keep this rule in view,
        Try, try again.

BYE-AND-BYE.

THERE is music enough in these three words for the burden of a song. There is hope wrapped up in them, an articulate beat of the human heart.

Bye-and-bye!

We heard it as long ago as we can remember, when we made brief but perilous journeys from chair to table, and from table to chair again.

We heard it the other day, when two parted that had been "loving in their lives," one to California, and the other to her her lonely home.

Everybody says it—sometime or another. The little boy whispers it when he dreams of exchanging the little stub shoes for boots like those of his father.

The man murmurs it — when in life's middle watch, he sees his plans half finished, and his hopes yet in the bud, waving in the cold late spring.

The old man says it—when he thinks of putting off the mortal for the immortal, to-day for to-morrow.

The weary watcher for the morning, whiles away the dark with "bye-and-bye."

Sometimes it sounds like a song; sometimes there is a sigh or sob in it. What wouldn't the world give to find it in almanacs—set down somewhere no matter, if in the dead of December—to know that it would surely come. But fairy-like as it is, flitting like a star-beam over the dewy shadows of years, nobody can spare it, and we look upon the many times these words have beguiled us.

FELTER S.

SUNSHINE.

SUNSHINE in the morning—
    Sunshine all the day—
Sunshine in the school-room—
    Sunshine out at play—
Sunshine in the workshop—
    Sunshine in the square—
Sunshine in the green lane—
    Sunshine every where.
Oh! 'tis sunshine ever

Around, within, above,
When the lips speak kindness,
And the heart breathes love.
Love is made of sunshine,
Kindness is all light,
These make joy of sorrow,
Noon-day of deep night.

OUR SCHOOL-TIME HOURS.

THOUGH summer's golden days are gone,
  And autumn's fruits and flowers,
We still have sunshine glowing here,
  Around our school-time hours.
And though we loved the pearly things,
  That gem'd the gay green sod,
'Tis here we learn that like ourselves,
  Their beauty comes from God.

He gives the winds and streams their songs,
  And in his goodness weaves,
O'er fragrant fields, and forest glades,
  Their bright-hued robes of leaves;
And there he gives our young hearts joy,
  Among their rich sweet scenes;
But here we learn in school-time hours,
  What all this goodness means.

We love the smiles he spreads o'er earth,
  For this to all they teach,
If earth is fair, how fairer far,
  Those realms we mean to reach.
We thank him, then, for school-time hours,
  And for the Sabbaths given,
And for their truths that lift our hearts
  From earth's joys up to heaven;

THE HOUSEHOLD "GOOD-NIGHT."

"GOOD-NIGHT!" A loud, clear voice from the
stairs said that—it was Tommy's. "Dood-
night!" murmurs a little something from the trundle-bed — a little something we call Jenny, that
filled a large place in the centre of one or two
pretty large hearts. "Good-night!" lisps a little
fellow in a plain rifle dress, who was christened
Willie about six years ago.

Now I lay me down to sleep,
I pray the Lord my soul to keep;
If I should die before I wake—

and the small bundle in the trundle-bed has dropped off to sleep; but an angel will finish the broken prayer, and it will go up sooner than many long-winded petitions that set out a great while before it.

And so it was " Good-night!" all around the homestead ; and very sweet music it made, too, in the twilight, and very pleasant melody it makes now, as we think of it, for it was not yesterday, nor the day before, but a long time ago—so long that Tommy is Thomas Somebody, Esq., and has forgotten that he ever was a boy, and wore what the bravest and richest of us can never wear but once if we try—the first pair of boots ; so long ago that Willie must stoop when he crosses the threshold : so long ago that Jenny has gone the way of the old prayer she was saying—for saying another. she did as before, fell asleep as she said it, and never waked more. Good night to thee, Jenny—good night!

And so it was good-night all around the house ; and the children had gone through the ivory gate, always left a little ajar for them—through into the land of Dreams ; or the golden one they call " Beautiful," into the land of Angels.

THE LIFE I'D LIVE.

THE life I'd live would be of faith
   Upon the Son of God,
Would see a "Thus the Lord hath said,"
   To guide me on the road.

The life I'd live would be to count
   All earthly gains but loss,
Would every day deny myself,
   And daily take my cross.

The life I'd live would be to mark
   The footsteps Jesus trod
To walk with care the narrow road
   That leads the soul to God.

The life I'd live would be to seek
   More earnestly his face.
Would grow in knowledge of my Lord,
   And daily grow in grace.

The life I'd live would be to live
   An humble, lowly life,
Far from the world's gay revelry
   And farther from its strife.

The death I'd die would be the death
   That's hidden in the Lord,
Dead to myself and dead to sin,
   But living through his word.

THE DEATH I'D DIE.

THE death I'd die would be to die
  With Jesus as my friend,
To know that pains and doubts and fears
  Had met their final end.

The death I'd die would be the death
  The Christian soldier dies;
In victory to yield my breath,
  And soar above the skies.

The death I'd die would be to sink
  Resignedly to rest,
Reclining on my Saviour's arms,
  My head upon his breast.

The death I'd die would be the death
  Which all the righteous die,
Blest of the Lord, their labors done,
  They rest with him on high.

The death I'd die, triumphantly
  With my last breath to sing,
Where is thy victory, O grave?
  And where, O Death, thy sting?

The death I'd die would be to have
  My Saviour near my bed,
To gently close my eyes, and sleep,
  With all the righteous dead.

CHARADE.

My first is a letter commanding to wed,
Or to lift your sole till it reaches your head ;
Nothing worth as a whole, it is plain to all men
That divided in halves, it is equal to ten ;

My second. though nothing, compared to the other,
Is worth more as a partner than its double-faced brother ;
It moans, and it sighs, and when joined to my first,
Pronounces the doom of the sinner accursed.

My third—you will find his whole value depends
On the worth and position of neighbors and friends.
And, when both the other two following fair,
Changes doom to desire, and a curse to a prayer.

My fourth, though it formeth no part of a hundred,
Shows where it can justly and evenly be sundered ;
'Tis found in all elements every where present,
'Tis found in all seasons, unpleasant or pleasant,
'Tis the chief of all lands, and yet cannot wait
On continent. hemisphere, empire or state.
Though ne'er in Great Britain suspected to lower,
Tis the heart of each quarter of that mighty power ;
It always belonged to the animal race,
In the mineral kingdom they gave it a place,
And, being impartial, they could not deny
The vegetable order its virtue to try ;
And yet, since creation. it never was known
In beast, bird, or fish, root, branch, stem or stone

My whole you'll find growing in pasture and barns,
Or grown in coats, carpets, warm blankets and yarns,

In England, in Saxony, France and old Wales
And in sundry more places it always prevails.
Of quadrupedal origin—still it is known
In bipedal families—oft it's been shown ;
But the strangest of all its strange forms and conditions
If seen in the covering of sage politicians.

-------- ♦♦♦ --------

WHAT IS A YEAR?

WHAT is a year? 'Tis but a wave
  On life's dark rolling stream.
Which is so quickly gone that we
  Account it but a dream.

'Tis but a single, earnest throb
  Of Time's old iron heart,
Which, tireless, now is strong as when
  It first with life did start.

What is a year? 'Tis but a turn
  Of Time's old brazen wheel ;
Or but a page upon the book
  Which death must shortly seal.

'Tis but a step upon the road
  Which we must travel o'er ;
A few more steps, and we shall walk
  Life's weary round no more.

THE DOGS IN THE PARLOR.

THE DOGS.

IN an extensive spinning and dye-work, in a town where I was at school two dogs were kept. One of them was a rather large size, the other quite small, and a cross, spiteful little animal it was. I do not now recollect their names, for it is almost thirty years since I knew them; but I shall call the largest one *Jowler*, and the other *Spot*, which I believe was really what his master called him. *Spot* was a pretty dog, and seemed so proud of being taken notice of, and allowed to rest himself on the office hearth-rug beside his master, and sometimes even to sit in the parlor at tea-time, and take scraps of the little children's bread or cake. that one would suppose he felt at liberty to behave rudely to *Jowler*, for he would snarl and bark when *Jowler* came near him, and seemed to want to keep their master's love all to himself. And, to tell the truth, no one was particularly fond of poor *Jowler*, who was only the yard watch-dog, kindly treated, but nothing more. One day that *Spot* was rambling about the yard, he carelessly missed his footing on a narrow path between the dye-pits, and fell into one of them. No person was near at the time; so poor *Spot* had to keep swimming from side to side, vainly trying to climb out. Alas! the sides were steep and smooth; there was no hold for even a little dog's paw; and he went round and round, and across again and

again, and began to feel quite tired of the cold
water. But no help came, though he cried out as
loudly as he could in his dog-talk, yelping and bark-
ing in a manner that told of his distress. Now the
larger dog was not far away, and no doubt he had
been listening all the while : but *Spot* had never
been kind to him, why should *he* be kind to *Spot ?*
Jowler never had been taught the "golden rule ;"
never had been bid to "love" his "enemies ;" and
poor *Spot* still shouted on, though now in a weaker
voice ! Just then, their master, who was a kind,
nice gentleman, entered the pit-yard, having heard
Spot's voice, and wondered what ailed him : and
there he saw *Jowler* quietly walk to the edge of the
pit, stretch himself at full length along the narrow
edge, bend over the side of the pit—(the water so
high that it brought *Spot* just within his reach)—
catch the little dog by the back of the neck, and
gently carry the poor dripping thing into a broad
safe place. Was not this good in *Jowler ?* And
Jowler's kind master did not forget it ; but always
after this took more notice of the faithful watch-dog,
and saw that he got many a nice bone to pick, for
the sensible way he saved the little one.

Now, is not this a pretty story ? and would not
every little boy and girl be glad to do a kindness in
the same way ? Yes ! I think every one would,
and I hope you will all try to do so, and never let
any one suffer, if any of you can prevent it.

But I have not yet told you what I think is the

best part of the story ; it is, that afterwards *Spot*
and *Jowler* were the best friends possible ! they used
to walk and run about, and sleep together ; and
Spot quite left off the rude habit of snarling at his
good friend ; so that *Jowler* found he had not merely
lost an enemy, but had also *gained a friend.*

We sometimes find that little kindnesses can be
shown by little children, as well as by little dogs,
and very often they lead to great benefits. But,
then, we must·not always look to the results ; but
do right simply because it *is right,* and because God
has commanded us to do all the good we can ; and
when next, dear mamma, or any one else who will
take the trouble, is at liberty to get the New Testa-
ment, ask her to show you, and learn each of you
the text which says, " To him that knoweth to do
good and doeth it not, to him it is sin."

———

" BUT did I tell what a time I had with my little
John ?"

" No , what was it ?"

" Why, I was showing him the martyrs thrown in
to the lions, and was talking very solemnly to him,
trying to make him feel what a terrible thing it
was. 'Ma! said he all at once, ' O ma !—just look
at that poor little lion away behind there—he won't
get any ' "

COLD WATER.

You may boast of your brandy and wine as you please,
   Gin. cider, and all the rest ;
Cold water transcends them in all the degrees,
   It is *good*—it is BETTER—'tis BEST,

It is good to warm you when you are cold,
   Good to cool you when you are hot ,
It is good for the young—it is good for the old,
   Whatever their outward lot.

It is better than brandy to quicken the blood,
   It is better than gin for the colic ,
It is better than wine for the generous mood,
   Than whiskey or rum for a frolic.

'Tis the best of all drinks for quenching your thirst,
   'Twill revive you for work, or for play ;
In sickness or health, 'tis the best and the first—
   Oh ! try it—you'll find it will pay.

A "STRANGE" PREACHER.

HIS name was Strange. Many will think his conduct was strange also. He was a zealous preacher, and a sweet singer. Nothing gave him so much pleasure as to go about the country preaching and singing. A benevolent gentleman, well off in worldly goods, desiring to make him and his family comfortable in their declining years, generously presented him a title-deed for three hundred and twenty acres of land. Strange accepted the donation with thankfulness, and went on his way, preaching and singing as he went. But after a few months he returned, and requested his generous friend to take the title-deed. Surprised at the request, the gentleman inquired—

"Is there any flaw in it?"

"Not the slightest."

"Is not the land good?"

"First rate."

"Isn't it healthy?"

"None more so."

"Why, then, do you wish me to take it back? It will be a comfortable home for you when you grow old, and something for your wife and children, if you should be taken away."

"Why, I'll tell you. Ever since, I've lost my enjoyment for singing. I can't sing my favorite hymn with a good conscience any longer.

" What is that ?"

" This :

> " ' No foot of land do I possess,
> Nor cottage in the wilderness,
> A poor wayfaring man.
>
> I dwell awhile in tents below,
> Or gladly wander to and fro,
> Till I my Canaan gain.
>
> Yonder's my house and portion fair,
> My treasures and my heart are there,
> And my abiding home.'

"There !" said Strange, "I'd rather sing that hymn than own America. I'd trust the Lord to take care of my wife and children."

He continued singing and preaching, and preaching and singing ; and the Lord, said the lecturer, did take care of him, and his shildren after him.

NOTHING is more easy than to grow rich. It is only to trust nobody, befriend none ; to heap interest upon interest, cent upon cent ; to destroy all the finer feelings of nature and be rendered mean, miserable, and be despised for some twenty or thirty years, and riches will come as sure as disease, disappointment, and a miserable death.

FARMER'S BOYS.

Out in every tempest,
  Out in every gale,
Buffeting the weather
  Wind, and storm, and hail;
In the meadow mowing,
  In the shady wood,
Letting in the sunlight
  Where the tall oaks stood.
Every fitting moment,
  Each skillful hand employs—
Bless me! were there ever
  Things like farmers' boys?

Though the palm be callous,
  Holding fast the plow,
The round cheek is ruddy,
  And the open brow
Has no lines and furrows
  Wrought by evil hours,
For that heart keeps wholesome,
  Trained in Nature's bowers,
Healthy, hearty pastime,
  The spirit never cloys
Heaven bless the manly
  Honest farmers' boys!

At the merry husking,
  At the apple bee,
How their hearts run over
  With genial harmless glee;
How the country maidens,
  Blush with conscious bliss,

At the love-word whispered,
    With a parting kiss;
Then the winter evenings,
    With their social joys!
Bless me! they are pleasant
    Spent with farmers' boys.

ADDRESS TO LAKE ERY.

Mity stream. How your bosom swells and *pants*,
And how you rip things. How wet you look, eh!
What "airs" you put on when you get to blow-
Ing! Yes—in September, how proud you are
'Cause you can raise the wind, and kick up **rows**
And fight the shore, and tear away lumber
Yards! (that is you used to onct.) But you're stopt.
How do you like that breakwater, you old fluid?
Doesn't that keep you respectable, and put
Straps on your *pants*. Don't that stick in your crop.
Didn't they give you "piles" when they put that there.
Why don't you try to fill up the canal,
I should think you would catch cold bein made
        Of such damp stuff.

        Who are you, any how?
What's going to come of you? You're found out—
You are going to leak out over the Falls.
That's it! You needn't be uppish cause you're
Nothing but rain water, in spite of your *bars*
You have to borry from other Lakes to keep
Yourself from gettin dry. Hey—you old bankrupt,
    Mity stream—adoo!

THE MERRY HEART

'Tis well to have a merry heart,
  However short we stay;
There's wisdom in a merry heart,
  Whate'er the world may say.
Philosophy may lift its head
  And find out many a flaw,
But give me the philosopher
  That's happy with a straw.

If life but brings us happiness,
  It brings us, we are told,
What's hard to buy, though rich ones try
  With all their heaps of gold;
Then laugh away, let others say
  Whate'er they will of mirth,
Who laughs the most may truly boast
  He's got the wealth of earth.

There's beauty in the merry heart,
  A moral beauty, too;
It shows the heart's an honest heart,
  That's paid each man his due;
And lent a share of what's to spare,
  Despite of wisdom's fears,
And makes the cheek less sorrow speak,
  The eye weep fewer tears.

The sun may shroud itself in cloud,
  The tempest wrath begin;
 t finds a spark to cheer the dark,
  Its sunlight is within;
Then laugh away, let others say
  Whate'er they will of mirth;
Who laughs the most may truly boast
  He's got the wealth of earth.

LITTLE RED RIDING-HOOD.

LITTLE RED RIDING HOOD.

EVERYBODY has read the story of this wonderful child. Of all the children of romance, she is perhaps the greatest favorite with very young readers. Can any one tell who wrote the story, and what gave rise to it?

Little Red Riding Hood was a very good girl. She was kind to every one, and loved everything. She was very kind to her old grandmother. She was willing to do anything for her father and mother. She was kind to the wasp, and to the tom-tit, and to the poor old woman whom she found seeking for water-cresses. She was even kind to the wolf, who, while men were near to protect her, appeared very amiable. But she was very weak and silly in believing what the wolf said, and holding conversation with him. And bitterly the poor child paid for it. She lost her good old grandmother, and would have lost her own life too, had not the friends which her kindness had made for her been near at hand to save her from the lying wolf.

Good children must beware of bad company. "Evil communications corrupt good manners," says the Bible, and flatterers are never true friends. They can not be safely trusted. You may be kind to everybody, even to the wicked, and to those who injure you. You can forgive them, and do them all the good you can. But you need not believe what they say, nor suffer yourself to be led astray by them.

THE CABIN BOY.

"PLEASE sir, don't you want a cabin boy?"

"I *do* want a cabin boy, my lad, but what's that to you? A little chap like you ain't fit for the berth."

"Oh, sir, I'm real strong. I can do a great deal of work, if I aint so very old."

"But what are you here for? You don't look like a city boy. Run away from home, hey?"

"Oh no indeed sir; my father died, and my mother is very poor, and I want to do something to help her. She let me come."

"Well, sonny, where are your letters of recommendation? Can't take any boys without those."

Here was a damper. Willie had never thought of its being necessary to have letters from his minister, or his teachers, or from some proper person, to prove to strangers that he was an honest and good boy. Now what *should* he do. He stood in deep thought, the captain meanwhile curiously watching the workings of his expressive face. At length he put his hand into his bosom, and drew out his little Bible, and without one word put it into the captain's hand. The captain opened it to the blank page and read:

"Willie Graham, presented as a reward for regular and punctual attendance at Sabbath School, and for his blameless conduct there and elsewhere. From his Sunday School Teacher."

Captain McLeod was not a pious man, but he could not consider the case before him with a heart unmoved. The little fatherless child, standing humbly before him, referring him to the testimony of his Sunday School teacher, as it was given in his little Bible, touched a tender spot in the heart of the noble seamen, and, clapping Willie heartily on the shoulder, he said : " You are the boy for me ; you shall sail with me ; and if you are as good a lad as I think you are, your pockets shan't be empty, when you go back to your mother."

"Who made you ?" inquired a lady teacher of a lubberly boy, who had lately joined her class.

" I don't know," said he,

" Don't know ! you ought to be ashamed of yourself—a boy fourteen years old ! Why there's little Dicky Filton—he is only three—he can tell, I dare say. Come here, Dickey ; who made you ?"

" Dod," lisped the infant prodigy.

" There," said the teacher triumphantly, " I knew he would remember,"

" Well, he oughter," said the stupid boy, " taint but a little while ago since he was made !"

THE REQUEST.

" FATHER, may I go down on the river, and hunt to-day?" asked a blue-eyed boy of about fifteen summers of his father.

"Roger, don't you know that I don't want you to go so far from home to hunt. I tell you now, never go there unless I or some other grown person accompany's you—and not then without my consent."

"Why, father, there is not no harm on the river is there, why don't you want me to go there?"

"Never mind, I have reasons; only you keep away from there."

Roger's father then left the house, and went up in town, where he generally passed his time. Soon after, about half a dozen boys stopped at the house of Roger.

"Halloa, Roger, get your gun and come on."

"Father won't let me go a hunting on the river," replied Roger.

"Well, come ahead, we aint going to hunt on the river," said one, winking at the others.

Roger took his gun and set out with the boys. Presently one of the boys asked one of his comrades how much farther it was to the river.

"Why," exclaimed Roger, "I thought you wasn't going to hunt on the river?"

"Well, we aint going to hunt on the *river*, but on its banks, ha, ha, ha."

Roger persisted against going, but they at last prevailed on him to accompany them, by laughing at him, calling him silly names, and telling him his father would never find it out.

While the boys were hunting, Roger discovered a turkey's track leading up the river. Slipping off from his comrades without being discovered, he followed the track. After going about half a mile up the river, looking ahead he saw about two hundred yards up the river, a turkey seated on a fallen tree. The turkey had not seen him, he kept on, taking care to keep out of the turkey's sight. Finding that his shoes made too much fuss he pulled them off. He was about to fire at the turkey, when he felt a sharp sting in his foot; looking down, to his horror, he saw a large Mockason snake under his feet. He had put his foot upon it, and it bit him. He shot the snake, and tying a string tight around his leg he ran towards home. He soon grew too weak to run. He cried for help, but was far from any house. He began to get so weak that he could not stand, he threw down his gun and crawled. At last he came to a road, and being exhausted, he sank down insensible. He had been bitten in the bottom of his foot by a poisonous snake. When he again woke to consciousness, he was upon a bed in his father's house. He had been found by a traveler soon after he fell exhausted in the road. He had escaped death indeed : but he had lost one of his limbs, which had to be cut off to prevent his death. He had a hair-breadth escape from the monster death, and was rendered a cripple for life, by one act of disobedience.

WHEN ONE WON'T QUARREL, TWO CAN'T.

WHEN boys are rude,
Or, in quarrelsome mood,
Throw stones, or strike, or fight—
To be gentle and kind
Is the way, you'll find,
To set matters quickly right,

BRILLIANTS.

THERE is dew for the flow'ret,
And honey for the bee,
And bowers for the wild bird,
And love for you and me!

There are tears for the many,
　And pleasures for the few;
But let the world pass on. dear,
　'There's love for me and you!

There's care that will not leave us,
　And pain that will not flee;
But in our hearts unaltered,
　Sits Love, 'tween you and me!

Our love, it ne'er was reckoned,
　Yet good it is, and true;
It's half the world to me, love,
　It's all the world to you!

———◆◆◆———

LITTLE THINGS.

Do something for each other—
　Though small the help may be,
There's comfort oft in little things
　Far more than others see!

It takes the sorrow from the eye,
　It leaves the world less bare,
If but a friendly hand come nigh
　When friendly hands are rare!

Then cheer the heart which toils each hour,
　Yet finds it hard to live;
And though but little in our power,
　That little let us give.

THE SUBLIME OF NONSENSE.

BY YOUNG ORATOR CLIMAX.

MOST illustrious litterati, and coadjutors :—On this imposing and awful occasion, in the midst of this mighty and terrible commotion of vast and capacious intellects, I usher myself into your august presence.

We are now witnessing the eruptive thunder of the human mind ; the ex-an-them'-a-tous and prodigious peals ever and anon bursting in the concave stellar deep.

We hear the reverberating echo from the craggy summits of the eternal mountains. My magnificient compeers, I shall pour forth the pure indivisible ef-flo-res'-en-ses—the huge massive performances— and the transcendent di-aph'-a-nous and perspicuous cog-i-ta-tions of one of the most brilliant and lofty geniuses that ever dwelt superincumbent amid the rich foliation and six-penny chicanery of our terrestrial emanation.

My di-das'-cal-ic faculties have expanded with singular pellucidness, and with a wonderful concatenation.

The number and variety of my ideas are incommensurable.

The flow of my intellectual efflux is incomparably tall and turbulent.

My mind is *hop-tu-cap'-su-lar—he-ro-i-comical* and

profound—free from the remotest approximation to egotistical ostentation ; humble, argumentative and insinuating. I delight in bold burning and sublime metaphors and met-an'-y-miss in the spiritual sciences of me-tem'-psy-cho-sis met-a-pas -co-py and sci-ag-ra-phy. I delight to revel amid postulates an-no-to'-tions on all oec-u-men'-i-cal om-ni-per-cip'-i-an-ces. The pandiculation of the universe is seen by perlus-tration and per-i'-grin-a-tion. I wish to make a short comprehensive oration, full of great principles and unsophisticated truths.

I desire not to blot my production with a trans-cursionary discussion of the doctrine of transelem-entation ; but introducing the utmost latitudinarian-ism into this wonderfully clear exergesis of the mysterious tide of human affairs. I desire to give my mind sea-room and expansion — or soar aloft amid the radiations and lofty effluxions and gener-alizations of the master spirits of the age. Standing here on the grand panorama of life, gazing aloft amidst the effulgent constellations of terrestrial im-mortal worthies, my soul is dilated to the extreme limits of metaphysical extension and restriction.

I feel the imposing and awful grandeur of my existence. I feel the high impulses stirring within my corruptible tabernacle ; the psychological movements of the mysterious spiritual machinery ; the impres-sive prognostications of immortality and the self-evident nonsemiperspicuous manifestations of the mental appurtenances.

I feel the lofty sublimity, the towering glory, the immense perfection of this glorious being.

Indeed I am filled with floods of overpowering emotions as I leave this listening audience.

NOT TIME ENOUGH.

NOT time enough? So the gilt edges of the Bible remain untarnished, and it leaves its own profile of dust on the table. Not time enough to study its teachings! But there is time enough for other things.

Time enough to coil around the soul the web of wealth, which, when completed, forms its shroud.

Time enough to amuse the fancy, to excite passion, to trifle with time, and to banish reflection.

Time enough to simmer away afternoon after afternoon in the maudlin sympathy of romantic sentimentalism, until the heart, in its voluptuous impotence, becomes incapable of real love to God or man!

Time enough to lay plot upon plot and scheme upon scheme for the gratification of ambition or vanity!

Time enough to be sick, though then, when the heart is troubled, and the body faint, and the head sluggish, there is indeed not time enough to repent!

TIME ENOUGH TO DIE.

ALL ABOUT EYES.

Blue eyes are tender,
  Blue eyes are true,
Blue eyes are lovely—
  Their smiles ever new.

Brown eyes are merry,
  Brown eyes are mild,
Brown eyes are beautiful
  As a fair child.

Brown eyes are dazzling
  When their orbs roll;
Brown eyes speak volumes
  Deep from the soul.

But black eyes are witching
  Black eyes are bright,

Black eyes are the index
Of the souls light.

Black eyes are glancing,
Black eyes are sweet,
Black eyes keep dancing,
When other's they meet.

———•••———

ANGRY WORDS.

Angry words are lightly spoken,
In a rash and thoughtless hour;
Brightest links of life are broken
By their deep, insidious power.
Hearts inspired by warmest feeling,
Ne'er before by anger stirr'd,
Oft are rent past human healing
By a single angry word.

Poisoned drops of care and sorrow,
Bitter Poison drops are they,
Weaving for the coming morrow
Saddest memories of to day!
Angry words, oh! let them never
From the tongue unbridled slip;
May the heart's best impulse ever
Check them ere they soil the lip!

Love is much too pure and holy,
Friendship is too sacred far,
For a moment's reckless folly,
Thus to desolate and mar.
Angry words are lightly spoken,
Bitterest thoughts are rashly stirred,
Brightest links of life are broken,
By a single angry word.

OUR LITTLE ANGEL.

SOME one has said, and wisely too, that " there is an angel in every house," though oft its inmates know it not. Methought the other day as I gazed on the face of " our Bertie," sleeping in quiet innocence in his cradle bed, that surely, an angel had taken up its abode with us. Who can gaze upon the sweet face and rose-bud lips of such a sleeper without feeling as if in the presence chamber of the

Diety, and that they are looking into an angel's face, so innocent, so pure, so holy :—a sweet lesson of immortality to all :—its young soul seems visible in each curve of its tiny fingers, each smile on its infant lips.

'The skeptic must here, in this sanctuary of purity, cease to cavil, the scoffer be hushed to silence, and the oaths of the profane all unuttered chill. —— Even "Old Pete," rough and untutored as he is, and so wicked too, halts while passing the door, to look on "our Bertie," exclaiming, "the little angel." Mother,—thine is a holy calling, a sacred trust is committed to thy keeping in that darling boy, "our Bertie," as you fondly call him. That beautiful, stainless soul is given thee to guard, to keep :—that angel, for thee to train for God and Heaven. Ponder well thine every word and look, thine every pressure of its tiny form, remembering that they each leave their impress on an angel's wing.

> Another little wave
>   Upon the sea of life :
> Another soul to save,
>   Amid its toil and strife.
>
> Two more little hands
>   To work for good or ill ;
> Two more little eyes ;
>   Another little will.
>
> Two more little feet
>   To walk the dusty road ;

To choose where two paths meet,
The narrow or the broad.

Another heart to love,
Receiving love again
And so the baby came,
A thing of joy and pain.

NUMBER OF STARS.

OF the stars thousands are visible to the naked eye and millions are discovered by the telescope. Sir John Herschell calculates that about five and a half millions of stars are visible enough to be distinctly counted in a twenty feet reflector in both hemispheres, and thinks that the actual number is much greater. His illustrious father estimated on one occasion that one hundred and twenty-five thousand stars passed through the field of his forty foot reflector in a quarter of an hour. This would give twelve millions for the entire circuit of the heavens in a single telescopic zone; and this estimate was made under the assumption that the nebulae were masses of luminous matter, not yet condensed suns. But with the increase of instrumental power, especially under the mighty grasp of Lord Rosse's gigantic reflector and the great reflector at Pulkova and Cambridge, the most irresolvable of these nebulae has given way; and the better opinion now is that every one of them is a galaxy, like our own milky way composed of millions of suns.

VOICES.

LISTEN to the roses,
Listen to the rills,
Listen to the breezes
Whispering o'er the hills.

They have each a burden
For the willing ear,
Saying to the listener,
God is ever near.

Listen to the rain drops,
Listen to the dew.
Listen to the sunshine
Whispering to you.

They are spirit voices,
Speaking to the heart—
Saying, God is near thee
Wheresoe'er thou art.

BY-AND-BY.

THERE'S a little mischief-making
Elfin, who is ever nigh,
Thwarting every undertaking,
And his name is By-and-By.

What we ought to do this minute,
"Will be better done," he'll cry,
"If to-morrow we begin it;"
"Put it off!" says By-and-By.

Those who heed his treacherous wooing,
Will his faithless guidance rue;
What we always put off doing,
Clearly we shall never do.

AN EVENING WITH PAPA.

"HERE comes papa!" exclaimed little Kate Elton, who had been standing sometime in the
library window to catch the first glimpse of papa's
hat when he should come home from the city. Edward! Susie!" she continued, "Here's papa coming,
make haste and come in. This is papa's evening
with us you know."

Edward and Susie were soon in the study ; and when Mr. Elton had seated himself comfortably in the easy chair, her little voice was heard again beseechingly, " Now, papa, a very pretty story tonight, if you please !"

" A very pretty story, Katie ?" replied Mr. Elton, " why, I think I have almost got to an end of all my stories. Shall I tell you what happened as I was coming home to night ?"

" Yes, do papa !" said Edward.

"As I was passing Lawrence Academy," began Mr. Elton, " the boys were just turning out, and one great boy was pushing right and left with such violence that finally he threw one little fellow against the iron gates, and hurt him very much. Upon this another boy came up, his eyes flashing with anger, and shouted, ' I say, Tom Harton, we won't allow you to be always pushing about in this way ; you're always knocking boys down ; you've hurt Fred Dinley very much. I shall tell the Doctor of you.'

" ' You tell the Doctor ! you cowardly fellow,' replied Tom Harton, ' what business is it of yours, pray ? You are always bullying me, and I won't stand it. We'll see which of us is master !' And he stood erect in a menacing attitude, which the other boy, whom I recognised as Will Langford, instantly assumed likewise. Mutual upbraiding was beginning again, and I doubt much if it would have

ended without blows, if I had not gone up and
made peace."

"How did you manage that, papa?" said Kate.

"It was no easy matter, I assure you, Katie.
When I stepped forward, I was met by such a
storm of complaints of rudeness from the one side,
and insolence from the other, that I feared I should
make but little way. At length I thought I would
relate to them a little incident which I witnessed
last week. I was standing in front of Beechbank
House when I espied through the bars of the garden
gate a frolicksome kitten at play. In its gambols it
chanced to come near a great whiskered Tabbie,
who apparently did not relish any such antics near
his dignified self; for he gave a hiss and a growl,
darted out a great pair of claws, patted and
scratched poor Kitty, and sent her away mewing.
Presently, however, she came back, bringing with
her her mother, a handsome white cat with a splendid tail, and the white cat and Tabbie began a regular fight, whilst Kitty sat by watching the pro-
ceedings with evident satisfaction.

When I had finished, I asked the boys if they did
not think their conduct in provoking and threaten-
ing one another bore great resemblance to the selfish
and revengeful spirit of the cats. They were silent,
but attentive; so I talked to them a little longer,
and told them that it was a very mistaken idea to
suppose that there was anything really manly in
acting in any way contrary to the true dignity of

man's nature, which consisted in his cultivating all
the higher and nobler faculties with which he was
so richly endowed, and which enjoined him to be
loving and gentle and considerate towards all. The
boys began to look rather ashamed, and Tom Harton muttered something about not having meant to
throw Dinley down, and Langford said in a very
different tone of voice from the one which he had
before assumed, 'I dare say you did not, but we
should be very much obliged to you, Harton, if you
would endeavor to be a little more polite.' This
produced a thaw ; peace was soon restored, and I
came home.

A LITTLE Swedish girl, while walking with her
father on a starry night, absorbed in contemplation
of the skies, being asked of what she was thinking,
replied, " I was thinking, if the *wrong side* of heav-
en is so glorious, what must the right side be !" Of
course, the wrong side, with her, was that which
looked on our lone and revolted earth. Surely, the
right side, that looks towards the throne of God and
the Lamb, must be beautiful exceedingly ! We do
not often meet with a thought so poetical and precious as this.

SONG OF THE TREE-TOAD.

"Once there was a tree-toad
Who lived in a tree;
He cared for nobody,
And nobody cared for he."
Old Song.

Up in a tree
Right merrily,
At close of day
I sing away
A tune of my own composition;
I don't care a fly
For passers by,
But keep right along
With my beautiful song—
A solo without any transition.

Some pretend to complain
They don't like my strain,
And think there should be variation;
But I continue still
With the same old trill,
And shall do so, in spite of all creation!

What do I care,
Up here in the air,
For the opinion of other people;
I am not dependent
Upon any attendant;
I'm as high as any church steeple!

Some think that my song
Is a hair too long,
And suggest now and then a cessation;
But I'll sing till I'm done,
If it takes till the sun
Has risen upon half the nation.

When I see a fuss,
And a very great muss
Round the base of my high habitation,
I simply look on,
And let it alone,
Growing wise by my keen observation.

I should feel very green
Should I ever be seen
Going round, making trouble among neigh-
    bors;
But I stay at home,
And never roam,
All content with domestic labors.

Let folks say what they will,
I shall always keep still,
And ne'er return evil for evil
For its no kind of use
To repay their abuse;
I shall always keep cool, calm and civil.

My character's such
That I don't care much,
If they pelt me with stones without reason;
For, up here in the tree,
I'm so hard to see,
That to find me, would take a whole season!

I'm a toad, in short,
That is hard to be caught,
And I can say, without any assumption,
That if all I see
Would imitate me,
They would show themselves men of *gump-
tion!*

For it seems very clear
To me, up here,
That the world would show far less remiss-
ness,
If every man,
So far as he can,
Like me, should *mind his own business!*

THE COMFORTS OF PLAYING "HOOKIE."

HAVE you any sympathy with this' poor boy? Do any of you see your own likeness here? Do you remember when you strayed away, after school, to have a slide, or a skating, on the pond, knowing all the while that your mother was expecting you home? Do you remember how, when it was near dark, and the snow began to fall thick and heavy, you started on your way home, half frozen, dissatisfied with yourself, and ready to cry with vexation, without finding anybody to be vexed with but yourself? Then you began to wish you had gone directly home from school—and then again, to wish, almost, that you had no home to go to, because you felt you ought to be punished, and feared you would be. You lingered along, growing colder and colder, instead of running briskly on, and warming yourself with the exercise. There is no fire that can make you so comfortable, in a cold day, as brisk, cheerful exercise. Ah! there was the mischief. You were not cheerful. You could not be cheerful for you had been doing wrong, and there is something in that to chill the body, as well as the spirit. Your fingers—how they smarted! Your ears—how they tingled! You tried blowing your fingers. Silly boy! do you not know that this only makes a bad matter worse? Beat them—thrash

THE 'BLOW.

them—rub them together—put them in your pockets, and run. Run home. Take a whipping, if it must be so, and resolve never to deserve another. But don't stand there, scaring yourself with such sorry looks, and hugging the cold, as it were your best friend. Hurry home at once, and —— what did you say? It was not you, eh? Well, I am glad of it. But pray who was it?

PLEASURE AND DUTY.

How men would mock at pleasure's shows,
Her golden promise, if they knew
What weary work she is to those
Who have no better work to do.

Curved is the line of beauty,
Straight is the line of duty;
Walk by the last, and thou shalt see
The other ever follow thee.

Oh! righteous doom, that they who make
Pleasure their only end;
Ordering their whole life for its sake,
Miss that whereto they tend.

While they who bid stern duty lead,
Content to follow, they,
Of duty only taking heed,
Find pleasure by the way.

TELLING MOTHER.

A CLUSTER of young girls stood about the door of the school-room, one afternoon, engaged in close conversation, when a little girl joined them, and asked what they were doing. "I am telling the girls a *secret*, Kate, and we will let you know, if you promise not to tell any one as long as you live," was the reply.

"I won't tell any one but my mother," replied Kate. "I tell her every thing, for she is my best friend."

"No, not even your mother, no one in the world,"

"Well, then I can't hear it; for *what I can't tell my mother is not fit for me to know.*" After speaking these words, Kate walked away slowly, and perhaps sadly, yet with a quiet conscience, while her companions went on with their secret conversation.

I am sure that if Kate continued to act on that principle, she became a virtuous, useful woman. No child of a pious mother will be likely to take a sinful course, if Kate's reply is taken as a rule of conduct.

As soon as a boy listens to a conversation at school, or on the play-ground, which he would fear or blush to repeat to his mother, he is in the way of temptation, and no one can tell where he will stop. Many a man dying in disgrace, in prison, or on the scaffold, has looked back with bitter remorse to the time when the first sinful companion gained his ear.

and came between him and a pious mother. Boys
and girls, if you would lead a Christain life, and
die a Christain death, make Kate's reply your rule:
" What I can not tell my mother, is not fit for me to
know ;" for a pious mother is your best friend.

POCKETS.—What about a youngster's dress is he
more proud of than his pockets ? Does his mother
forget to insert a pocket in his apron, she is quickly
reminded of it, and obtains no peace until the omis-
sion is supplied. What mother ever finished her
boy's first pantaloons without a pocket on either
side. And with his legs encased in the little cloth
tubes, as he struts off, where are his hands? Has
his mother lost her thimble, where can she find it ?
Is any thing ever suffered to lie loose on the floor,
small enough to go into his pocket? And at a later
stage of life, when the world's good begin to attract
his attention, and that decidedly human nature com-
mences stealing over him, and his pockets are larger, and he has more of them, are they less used ?
Let the following exposition answer. A mother
in a neighboring village, says she emptied her hopeful son's pocket, the other day, and the following
articles were brought to light : Sixteen marbles, one
top, an oyster shell, two pieces of brick, one dough
nut, a piece of curry comb, one paint brush, three
wax ends, a handful of corn, a chisel, two broken
knives, a skate strap, three buckles, one ball, two
primers, five hen's eggs, and a bird's nest.

TELL-TALE FACE.

I HATE those frigid notions,
　　That seem to count it sin,
To show the kind emotions
　　True feeling wakes within.
Those manners cold, and guarde
　　With words dealt out by rule,
Pronounced just as mamma did,
　　Or Madam F—— at school.

I love the playful fancies
　　Of an unsuspecting heart,
That speak, in songs and glances
　　Unchecked by rules of art.
I love the face that speaketh
　　Of all that's in the mind;
The brow, the eye, that taketh
　　Its hue from what's behind.

This voice is none but Nature's—
　　The language of the soul,
Words err; but o'er the features
　　Guile may not have control.
The tongue can tell of feelings
　　That *may be*, or may not;
But the eye hath sure revealings
　　Of the deeply-hidden thought.

I love the quick expression
　　That flashes the full eye,
When truth would make confession,
　　Whilst modesty would lie.

Those warm. those heavenly blushes,
  That kindle brow and cheek,
When feeling's fountain gushes
  With what it dare not speak.

Those shades that come unbidden,
  With every passing cloud ; ·
Which tell of care, deep hidden
  'Mid merry looks, or proud.
That sudden gleam of pleasure
  From brow, and eye, and lip,
Which tell the heart has treasure
  It scarce knows how to keep.

These, these are voices given
  For soul to speak with soul
As true to truth and Heaven
  As the needle to the pole.
I bow to wit, and beauty,
  And I almost worship grace,
But I owe a special duty
  To an honest tell-tale face.

THE SUSPENSHIN BRIDGE AT NIAGARY.

Anormous structur ! Whar, Ide like to know,
Did the constructors stand as bilt this rode
Rite throo the air ? Say, gentle mews,
Wot hed they to hold on to ? But, alas !
The mews sez nuthin'. Oh, Jerewsalem !
Wot boyed them up ! Imadjinashin flored,
Can't git the hang of it !
              I hev it now !
They did it in balloons !

THE STONE IN THE POND.

THERE goes the stone, splash in the pond! Look at the circles round the place where it went in! —They grow larger and larger, till they fill the whole pond!

Our heart is like the pond. Every thought, every word we utter, every action, is a stone thrown into it. It may seem a small matter to say that little word, or to think that little thought, or to do that little action : but we must not despise little things ; for there is nothing so trifling but it may be very serious.

A boy once slyly took a marble from his playmate, while he was playing with him : but, as he did not notice his loss, it was not known. Soon after, the same boy took some cake from his mother's cupboard ; but she did not find it out. Next he stole some money from his father ; but he did not miss it. He then robbed his master : and at last it was found out, and he was taken to prison, and sent far away to a strange land. and he never saw his father and mother again. Perhaps. if he had not cheated his playmate of the marble, he would never have robbed his master, and come to so bad an end. He did not think that the little stone would produce first a small circle, then a larger one, and at last ruin his good name.

Watch over the first steps ; think no sins little ; be afraid of evil in the bud ; and good books, good advice, and, above all, God's good Spirit, will be stones thrown into the pool of your heart, to bless and save you.

———

A very excellent lady sought to instruct her grandchild in relation to the provident care of Heaven.

" Who gives you your daily bread ?" asked she.

" Dod," replied the child ; " but uncle Peter puts the butter and sugar on."

HISTORY OF A FLOWER.

WHEN the world was first created, when God
said " let there be light," when, at his bidding
the flowers sprang up, and the trees put forth their
leaves, and the green grass crept up the hill-side,
then I was born in a quiet place under a large ash
tree in the very heart of a thick forest.

And there I lived and grew unnoticed. Years
flew by, and every winter I dropped my leaves, and
remained for months buried in the snow ; and every

spring put on a robe of green and bloomed in soli-
tude. Very near my sylvan home a brook ran slowly
along, seeming like a beautiful mirror, as it reflected the tall trees that rose above it and the fair
flowers that bent over it. I had often wished to be
one of those favored flowers whose roots were
nourished by the waters, and who could see their
beauty reflected in them, for though I had lived
long, I did not know whether my form was beautiful or not. While I was vainly wishing that I had
been born by the brookside, I saw a gentleman
walking through the woods : he seemed to be fond of
flowers, for he carried many in his hand, to which
he added others as he passed along. He appeared
delighted with the quiet beauty of the place. At
first he did not notice me, but when his attention
was drawn that way, he seemed surprised : I did
not know that he was admiring my simple beauty.
He took a small spade which he carried, and carefully loosened the earth about my roots, and drew
me from the spot where so many happy hours had
been spent. He wrapped large leaves around me to
shelter me from the sun, and went from the wood
into the open field, and after walking for some time
he stopped before a poor but neat cottage. He went
in, and addressing a young woman who was rock-
ing in a large arm-chair and looking very pale, he
said, "Mary, I have brought you this beautiful
flower."

Mary received me gratefully, and placed me in a

glass of water, saying that she would ask her husband to plant me when he came home; the gentleman then took his leave. I was soon placed in a
flower-pot and lived in the cottage for some years.
Here I was happier than before; it was true I often
sighed for the pure air, and mossy couch on which I
reclined in the beautiful quiet of my old home, but I
was soon consoled by the thought that I now
bloomed for the happiness of others. I brought a
smile to the face of the invalid as I budded and
opened my beauties before her, and I endeavored to
repay her care by shedding my perfume in the sick-
chamber.

But time brought its changes. A lovely child
had been born there, and I saw that the mother was
gradually passing away. She died, and her husband
soon followed her to the spirit-land. Their son,
thus left an orphan, was taken by his uncle, who
was a poor man with a large family, and therefore
looked upon the boy with an unfriendly eye, and
sometimes treated him unkindly. One dark night he
let himself down from a window and ran away, still
carrying me with him. After walking for some time
he came to a large city, where he went into the
market and with much sorrow he offered me for
sale, for he was penniless. My rare beauty drew
many admirers, but all refused to pay the exorbitant
price demanded. At last, however, a rich gentleman purchased me. He took me to a fine house
where he showed me to his wife; she admired me

very much. I was then given to the gardener with directions for planting me by a fountain where I now am. Here in this lovely spot, the companion of the most gorgeous flowers, beside this crystal fountain, whose tinkling sound mingling with the rustling of the breeze makes "music soft and low," one would think I could ask nothing more. 'Tis true I love these bright flowers, but the bright cheek and lips of the invalid were dearer to me, for I felt that I was her consoler. I love this crystal fountain that waters me, but dearer far were the tears of that orphan boy, for as they dropped on my leaves I threw back my sweetest perfume to revive his drooping spirit; I awakened memories of his sainted mother; I made him happy. Thus, as we strew blessings along the pathway of the sorrowing, so are we made happy in return.

LIFE'S SMILES.

LIFE! ah! what is it? illusive and bright;
An angel's brief visit in a halo of light?
Ah! who shall define it, and what may it be?
A light dancing shallop on time's silver sea?
A flood of warm sunlight shed down from on high?
A moonbeam's soft glow, from a star-spangled sky?
A meteor's glare in the darkness of night,
Or lightning's quick flash, evanescent and bright°
An eagle's strong wing, dashing quickly away,
Or soaring more proudly in quest of his prey?
A mist that may rise to the thunder-bolt's berth,
Or sink and dissolve in the bogs of the earth?
O, tell us what is it, ye sages—who knows
From whence is its coming, and whither it goes?

A rainbow, whose splendor, the vision may lure,
With tints all too beautiful long to endure?
A dew-spangled morn—a fair summer flower,
Whose glories evanish and fade in a hour?
A zephyr—a tempest—a torrent—a pool?
A quiet—a tumult—a lesson—a school?
A fleeting probation—a shifting of scene?
A mystification—and what does it mean?
A pleasure exquisite—a medley—a pain—
O, say you what is it?—I pray you explain,
Ye that have kenn'd of it, silence forego.
What is the end of it? tell if ye know.

Mortal! list, and you shall hear.
Life's a joy and life's a tear:
Quickly o'er, or wiped away:
Soon is closed, its transient day.
Life is fleeting,
Life is free;
Life's a shallop on time's sea.

Life's a shadow,
Life is bright,
Life's a halo,
Life is light:
Life's a sunbeam from on high,—
Moonlight in a starry sky.
Life's a meteor of the night;
Life is lightning—quick and brigh
Life's an eagle—swift of wing;
Life's a brief—a transient thing.
Life's a mist, destined to soar,
Or to sink and rise no more!
Life's a rainbow,
Life's a dew;
Life has tints of every hue.
Life's a vision,
Life's a dream,
Life's a tumult,
Life's a theme,
Life's a zephyr,
Life's a flower,
Life may vanish in an hour.
Life's a torrent,
Life's a pool,
Life's a lesson,
Life's a school;
Life's a tempest,
Life's a calm,
Life's a blessing,
Life's a balm:
Life's a drama,
Life's a scene,
Life is shifting,
Life is lean,
Life's a struggle,

Life's a breath
And the end of life is death.
Such is life's history—soon it is o'er.—
Solved is its mystery—conn'd is its lore.

*   *   *   *   *   *

Is *that* the whole of it,
    Ever and anon.
Body and soul of it
    Going and gone?

Fondest hopes blasting!
    Oh! horrible theme!
Is life everlasting
    A fanciful dream?

Is there no hope for us,
    Merciful God!
But a lone scope for us
    Under the sod?

Is there not grace for us,
    Father of love!
Room for us, place for us
    With thee above?

Are there not mansions
    Prepared for the just?
God of salvation!
    In thee is our trust!

Jesus hath died for us,
    He hath the power;
He shall decide for us
    In the dark hour.

Our cares on him casting
    Shall lighten our gloom!
And to life everlasting,
    Will rise from the tomb.

Then shall life's history
  Never be o'er,
Resolving its mystery
  In eternity's lore.

*   *   *   *

Then life is a blessing—
  A boon from above—
A gift worth possessing,
  A token of love.

Whoso neglecteth it,
  Proves a bad liver;
Whoe'er rejecteth it
  Spurneth the giver.

Take it with gratitude;
  Cherish it, care for it;
Crave you beatitude?
  You must prepare for it.

Waste not your energies,
  Toiling for Mammon:
False is the idol
  As Jupiter Ammon.

Are you in thraldom?
  You must come out of it,
That we may all come,
  There is no doubt of it:

Nothing restrictory
  Crosses the road—
Press on to victory,
  Children of God!

To love and love's labor
  Then limit your strife;
Be God and your neighbor
  The joy of your life.

THE INDIAN.

WANTS HIS LAND-WARRANT.

WHILE the Creek war was raging, a portion of those Indians were friendly to the whites, and have received bounty land warrants for their services ; but occasionally one on the wrong side of the question puts in his claim, most ignorantly, but with great faith in getting it.

A short time since a renowned Hajo of the Creek nation requested the services of one of our attorneys while traveling in the Indian country, in procuring his land warrant from the Department. The lawyer was delighted at the prospect of a good fee ; the Indian promising him half the worth of the warrant, in the event of it being obtained. The lawyer wished to know of his employer the services he had rendered.

"Don't know talk like this," said the astonished Indian.

" Well, who did you fight under ?" continued the lawyer.

"Me fight under log," said Hajo.

" No, no ; but who was your captain ?" the lawyer inquired.

" Me big man, me captain too," answered the Indian.

" I want to know where you fought," said the lawyer, " at what battle ?"

" Me fight big heap, me shoot behind tree, me shoot under bank river. shoot big gun heap," said the Indian.

" Well, what did you shoot at," asked the lawyer, thinking that he would defer further questions till an interpreter could be procured.

" *Me shoot at Gineral Jackson, tree, four times,*" replied the warrant seeker.

ROSE AND THE FLOWER.

" ROSE, my pet," said Mr. Morton to his little girl, "why are you plucking so many flowers ?"

"To take to auntie, papa. I am sure she will like them, they are such beauties."

"Aunt has finer of her own, love."

"Then I may keep them for myself ; may I not ? They will refresh us on the road."

A kind smile said, "Yes ;" and happily did little Rose spring into the car.

When they came to the station, Rose saw many people outside. Among them, were some poor, wretched-looking children, thin and dirty. They looked very hard at Rose and her bright nosegay ; and one of them at last took courage to say, "Please give me a flower !"

Now, she was often called a kind little girl ; but this time, I am sorry to say, she did not deserve the name : for, thinking, "How can I give my pretty fuschia and jessamine, and these lovely carnations, to these dirty little creatures," she ran after her papa into the station.

At last, the train went off ; but Rose, although she had been busy watching the engines, could not make herself quite easy about her flowers and the poor children, though she tried to excuse herself by

thinking, " Oh ! they could never have taken care oɪ
them, so it would have been no good to have given
them away."

At the next station, there came into the carriage
where Rose was, a little cripple, who looked pale
and ill. Some one, whom Rose thought was her
mother, stood outside, saying, with tears, "Good-
bye ! God bless my poor child !" and a lady came
to the window and gave her a flower—a geranium.
Such a beautiful one ! Rose's eyes were fixed on it
directly. It seemed to please the child, too, for she
said, " Thank you, Miss Lucy ! Oh, it *is* pretty !"

The train started, and the child kept her eyes,
which were full of tears, fixed on her mother, till
she could see her no more, and then she looked at
her flower, so fondly ! and turned it every way,
that she might see all its beauty.

Not for some time did she see Rose, who was
watching her earnestly.

" That lovely geranium !" thought Rose ; "how
much more beautiful it is than any of my flowers !"
and she looked at her own now despised nosegay.

At last they came to another station. The little
cripple moved slowly to the other end of the seat,
opposite Rose. She bent forward, and said, in a
pleasant voice, " I think you like my flower ; do
take it ?" Rose blushed, for she did not know that
her looks had told her wishes so plainly. She
thought, " How good this poor child is ! Her only
flower, too !" But she had yet said nothing, and the

poor cripple felt sad, thinking she had offended Rose. At last Rose said, " No, I thank you ; I have all these of my own."

Her father had watched what passed anxiously, for he feared Rose would take the flower. But, instead of that, she moved up to him, whispering, " Papa, this little girl loves flowers ; may I give her mine!" He smiled a glad answer, and Rose carefully took up her nosegay, and laid it on the child's lap, and then went back quickly to her papa. The little girl thanked Rose, but would only take one or two.

Mr. Morton began to talk to her, and found that she was going to her aunt's at Leamington, as the doctor advised it ; and she thought that if she tried to make wax-flowers, some of the ladies might buy them, for her mother was poor.

Rose never forgot the lesson she had taught her, and was always after that kind herself and tried to make others so.

TOP PHILOSOPHY.

CHILDREN must be busy,
  Always something learning.
Toys and trinkets, for their secrets,
  Inside-outward turning.

While the top is spinning,
  Boys are wondering all.
How it stands erect unaided,
  Why it does not fall.

While the top is humming,
  Still the wonder grows,
By what art the little spinner
  Whistles as it goes.

Children learn while playing;
  Children play while learning;
Pastimes, often more than lessons,
  Into knowledge turning.

www.ingramcontent.com/pod-product-compliance
Lightning Source LLC
Chambersburg PA
CBHW030405270326
41926CB00009B/1282